Fiery Faith

Fiery Faith

Ignite Your Passion for God

A.W. Tozer

Compiled by W.L. Seaver

WingSpread Publishers
Camp Hill, Pennsylvania

WingSpread Publishers
Camp Hill, Pennsylvania
www.wingspreadpublishers.com

A division of Zur Ltd.

Fiery Faith
ISBN: 978-1-60066-299-7
LOC Control Number: 2011945936
Compilation, Preface and Questions
© 2012 by William L. Seaver

All A.W. Tozer excerpts are © Zur Ltd and
published by WingSpread Publishers.

16 15 14 13 12   5 4 3 2 1

Cover design by Pencil Tip Design

Contents

Preface

Unlike some others who have compiled Tozer's works, I never knew the man personally. However, I have been reading Tozer's writings for at least forty years, and I reread many of them every year. (My philosophy is to never buy a book unless it is worth reading over and over, and not many Christian books meet that standard if one is serious about growing in Christ.) As such, my forty-plus years of pouring over his words, praying, observing the saints and studying the Scriptures concerning the things that Tozer said and wrote has made me very familiar with the man and the insights he gleaned from the Word of God.

My own writings reflect his influence. For instance, Tozer has a powerful essay, "Faith Is a Journey, Not a Destination," in *Born After Midnight*. Using the text from Acts 2:42 ("They were continually devoting themselves to the apostles' teaching and to fellowship, to the breaking of bread and to prayer"), he writes,

> Conversion for those first Christians was not a destination; it was the beginning of a journey. And right there is where the Biblical emphasis differs from ours. . . . In the book of Acts, faith was for each believer a beginning, not an end; it was a journey, not a bed in which to be waiting for the day of our Lord's triumph.

Not many authors talk about the faith journey, but it should come as no surprise that a recent book of mine has the faith journey as a major theme. *A Mosaic of Faith: 11 Lessons Jesus Taught His Disciples* (WingSpread Publishers, 2012) looks at the faith journey from Jesus' perspective during the last two years of His ministry. Tozer was definitely ahead of the times with his divine insights on faith.

On another occasion, in "Errors in Thinking" from *Rut, Rot or Revival*, Tozer made the following observation from the divine perspective on the nature of the church:

> You see, the church is a body of individuals united in Christ but having separate individual responsibilities. Thus, the body is improved only as we improve the individuals that compose the body.

The implication of this comment is that the faith of the individuals in the local church or Christian ministries must grow for that institution to grow in faith as well. Our faith is "more precious than gold" (1 Peter 1:7) and is being tested and refined by God. His shepherds on earth are co-shepherds with Him and are to feed the flock, lead them to rest, strengthen the weak, heal the sick, bind up the injured, bring back the strays and search for the lost (Ezekiel 34:2–4, 15–16). All of this is to be done with humility, in faith and in love. Domination of the sheep by force and severity is the way of the flesh.

Many saints feel that the generation coming after them does not know the Lord, or the works of the Lord, nor the true essence of walking by faith in Him in everything we do. In that light, this compilation of Tozer's works on faith has come together.

Of course, walking by faith in God permeated everything Tozer wrote, which made it difficult to limit the selection, since so many of his writings pertain to faith. Had I chosen only essays with the word *faith* in the title, however, only ten of the thirty writings would have been included in the compilation. To avoid these alternate options of too much and too little, it was decided to include only those writings that address one or more specific issues of faith.

The ordering of the thirty writings was difficult as well. Grouping them by the Tozer books they originally came from misses the process or journey of faith that Tozer taught. The ordering of the writings in this compilation, therefore, begins with a Godward focus ("Following Hard After God" from *The Pursuit of God*) and ends there as well ("The Gaze of the Soul" from *The Pursuit of God*). In addition, the thirty writings are arranged in five sextuplets. The reason for this ordering was to provide flexibility, for both individual and group study.

The first sextuplet has a strong focus on the character of God, the second on the journey of faith, the third on the action of faith, the fourth on realities of faith and the fifth on hard issues of faith. This allows one to work through one sextuplet on one particular topic, choose one writing from each of the sextuplets, or use it like a devotional, going through one writing each day for a month. There are many ways to use the ordering to see your faith in God revived and refreshed.

"And without faith it is impossible to please Him, for he who comes to God must believe that He is and that He is a rewarder of those who seek Him" (Hebrews 11:6). It should be obvious that we cannot know God by sight but only by faith, and faith in Him alone in all that we do and think pleases Him. Tozer had more deep and timely things to say about faith than any other author I know. The life of faith is not an easy life. The path of faith is splashed with uncertainty, dry spells, difficult situations, the unknown, the hiding of God, mountain and valley experiences, poor and perfect timing, euphoria and discouragement and much more. However, no matter how tough things get, God is always there and waiting on us to depend upon Him only.

One of the great difficulties in the life of faith is that things are not always what they appear to be. Success could be by faith or by the flesh. On the other hand, failure is usually thought of as always being by the flesh and not by faith—but Scripture tells us otherwise! Jeremiah preached to his generation in the power of the Spirit, but from a human perspective he appeared to be an utter failure because the nation refused to repent.

David is considered to be "a man after His own heart" (1 Samuel 13:14 ; see Acts 13:22). He had lots of projects that he undertook under God's leading. One such project that took about a year and in the end was successful was the taking of the royal city of the Ammonites, Rabbah (2 Samuel 11:1–2; 12:26–31). During that year's time, David had been guilty of adultery, deception, cover-up, murder of Uriah (Bathsheba's husband) and a mass killing of Uriah's comrades at the wall. The project was finished successfully, but when one looks at the carcasses of lives along the road, it is evident that it was not done by faith. In fact, the instances of this year affected David the rest of his life, even though he confessed his sin.

Another instance of appearances comes from Numbers 20, where God tells Moses to speak to the rock for water to come forth; but Moses in anger strikes the rock. Water comes forth abundantly to meet the needs of the congregation and the beasts (Numbers 20:11), but God is very displeased by the disobedience of Moses. From the people's perspective, it was a success, but from God's perspective it was a failure because it wasn't done God's way, which is by faith. Thus, results can be deceiving without the divine perspective.

It is my prayer that God will use this compilation of Tozer's writings on faith and the questions for reflection or discussion at the end of each chapter to draw you closer to Him, to jump-start your faith in God, to increase your hunger for His Word and to purify your service to others. The journey starts in the first writing, "Following Hard after God," where He has put that urge within us to spur us on this divine pursuit and where He has provided the empowerment for this pursuit as well. The journey comes full circle in the last writing, "The Gaze of the Soul," where Tozer notes that "faith is the continuous gaze of the heart at the Triune God." There are two prayers at the end of the last writing, one by Tozer and one by myself, that should be the prayer of your heart. As you pray, read, meditate, study and pray more in the power of the Holy Spirit every day, you will begin to know the exciting journey of faith for which God redeemed you!

CHARACTER OF GOD

Chapter 1

Following Hard after God

My soul followeth hard after thee: thy right hand upholdeth me. (Psalm 63:8)

Christian theology teaches the doctrine of prevenient grace, which, briefly stated, means that before a man can seek God, God must first have sought the man.

Before a sinful man can think a right thought of God, there must have been a work of enlightenment done within him. Imperfect it may be, but a true work nonetheless, and the secret cause of all desiring and seeking and praying that may follow.

We pursue God because, and only because, He has first put an urge within us that spurs us to the pursuit. "No man can come to me," said our Lord, "except the Father which hath sent me draw him" (John 6:44), and it is by this prevenient *drawing* that God takes from us every vestige of credit for the act of coming. The impulse to pursue God originates with God, but the outworking of that impulse is our following hard after Him. All the time we are pursuing Him, we are already in His hand: "Thy right hand upholdeth me."

In this divine "upholding" and human "following," there is no contradiction. All is of God, for as von Hügel teaches, *God is always previous*. In practice, however (that is, where God's previous working meets man's present response), man must pursue God. On our part there must be positive reciprocation if this secret drawing of God is to eventuate in identifiable experience of the divine. In the warm language of personal feeling, this is stated in Psalm 42:1–2: "As the hart panteth after the water brooks, so panteth my soul after thee, O God. My soul thirsteth for God, for the living God: when shall I come and appear before God?" This is deep calling unto deep, (see 42:7) and the longing heart will understand it.

The doctrine of justification by faith—a biblical truth, and a blessed relief from sterile legalism and unavailing self-effort—has in our time fallen into evil company and been interpreted by many in such a manner as actually to bar men from the knowledge of God. The whole transaction of religious conversion has been made mechanical and spiritless. Faith may now be exercised without a jar to the moral life and without embarrassment to the Adamic ego. Christ may be "received" without creating any special love for Him in the soul of the receiver. The man is "saved," but he is not hungry nor thirsty after God. In fact, he is specifically taught to be satisfied and is encouraged to be content with little.

The modern scientist has lost God amid the wonders of His world; we Christians are in real danger of losing God amid the wonders of His Word. We have almost forgotten that God is a person and, as such, can be cultivated as any person can. It is inherent in personality to be able to know other personalities, but full knowledge of one personality by another cannot be achieved in one encounter. It is only after long and loving mental intercourse that the full possibilities of both can be explored.

All social intercourse between human beings is a response of personality to personality, grading upward from the most casual brush between man and man to the fullest, most intimate communion of which the human soul is capable. Religion, so far as it is genuine, is in essence the response of created personalities to the creating personality, God. "This is life eternal, that they might know thee the only true God, and Jesus Christ, whom thou hast sent" (John 17:3).

God is a person, and in the deep of His mighty nature, He thinks, wills, enjoys, feels, loves, desires and suffers as any other person may. In making Himself known to us, He stays by the familiar pattern of personality. He communicates with us through the avenues of our minds, our wills and our emotions. The continuous and unembarrassed interchange of love and thought between God and the soul of the redeemed man is the throbbing heart of New Testament religion.

This intercourse between God and the soul is known to us in conscious personal awareness. It is personal: It does not come through the body of believers, as such, but is known to the individual, and to the body through the individuals that compose it. It is conscious: it does not stay below the threshold of consciousness and work there unknown to the soul (as, for instance, infant baptism is thought by some to do), but comes within the field of awareness where the man can know it as he knows any other fact of experience.

You and I are in little (our sins excepted) what God is in large. Being made in His image, we have within us the capacity to know Him. In our sins we lack only the power. The moment the Spirit has quickened us to life in regeneration, our whole being senses its kinship to God and leaps up in joyous recognition. That is the heavenly birth without which we cannot see the kingdom of God. It is, however, not an end but an inception, for now begins the glorious pursuit, the heart's happy exploration of the infinite riches of the Godhead. That is where we begin, I say, but where we stop no man has yet discovered, for there is in the awful and mysterious depths of the Triune God neither limit nor end.

Shoreless Ocean, who can sound Thee?
Thine own eternity is round Thee,
Majesty divine!

To have found God and still to pursue Him is the soul's paradox of love, scorned indeed by the too easily satisfied religionist, but justified in happy experience by the children of the burning heart. St. Bernard stated this holy paradox in a musical quatrain that will be instantly understood by every worshipping soul:

We taste Thee, O Thou Living Bread,
And long to feast upon Thee still:
We drink of Thee, the Fountainhead
And thirst our souls from Thee to fill.

Come near to the holy men and women of the past and you will soon feel the heat of their desire after God. They mourned for Him, they prayed and wrestled and sought for Him day and night, in season and out, and when they had found Him the finding was all the sweeter for the long seeking. Moses used the fact that he knew God as an argument for knowing Him better. "Now therefore, I pray thee, if I have found grace in thy sight, shew me now thy way, that I may know thee, that I may find grace in thy sight" (Exodus 33:13); and from there he rose to make the daring request, "I beseech thee, shew me thy glory" (33:18). God was frankly pleased by this display of ardor, and the next day called Moses into the mount, and there in solemn procession made all His glory pass before him.

David's life was a torrent of spiritual desire, and his psalms ring with the cry of the seeker and the glad shout of the finder. Paul confessed the main-spring of his life to be his burning desire after Christ. "That I may know him" (Philippians 3:10), was the goal of his heart, and to this he sacrificed everything. "Yea doubtless, and I count all things but loss for the excellency of the knowledge of Christ Jesus my Lord: for whom I have suffered the loss of all things, and do count them but dung, that I may win Christ" (3:8).

Hymnody is sweet with the longing after God, the God whom, while the singer seeks, he knows he has already found. "His track I see and I'll pur-sue," sang our fathers only a short generation ago, but that song is heard no more in the great congre-gation. How tragic that we in this dark day have had our seeking done for us by our teachers. Every-thing is made to center upon the initial act of "ac-cepting" Christ (a term, incidentally, which is not found in the Bible) and we are not expected there-after to crave any further revelation of God to our souls. We have been snared in the coils of a spurious logic, which insists that if we have found Him, we need no more seek Him. This is set before us as the last word in orthodoxy, and it is taken for granted that no Bible-taught Christian ever believed otherwise. Thus the whole testimony of the worshipping, seeking, singing church on that subject is crisply set aside. The experiential heart-theology of a grand army of fragrant saints is rejected in favor of a smug interpretation of Scripture that would certainly have sounded strange to an Augustine, a Rutherford or a Brainerd.

In the midst of this great chill, there are some, I rejoice to acknowledge, who will not be content with shallow logic. They will admit the force of the argument, and then turn away with tears to hunt some lonely place and pray, "O God, show me Thy glory." They want to taste, to touch with their hearts, to see with their inner eyes the wonder that is God.

I want deliberately to encourage this mighty longing after God. The lack of it has brought us to our present low estate. The stiff and wooden quality about our religious lives is a result of our lack of holy desire. Complacency is a deadly foe of all spiritual growth. Acute desire must be present or there will be no manifestation of Christ to His people. He waits to be wanted. Too bad that with many of us He waits so long, so very long, in vain.

Every age has its own characteristics. Right now we are in an age of religious complexity. The simplicity that is in Christ is rarely found among us. In its stead are programs, methods, organizations and a world of nervous activities that occupy time and attention but can never satisfy the longing of the heart. The shallowness of our inner experience, the hollowness of our worship and that servile imitation of the world that marks our promotional methods all testify that we, in this day, know God only imperfectly, and the peace of God scarcely at all.

If we would find God amid all the religious externals, we must first determine to find Him, and then proceed in the way of simplicity. Now, as always, God discovers Himself to "babes" and hides Himself in thick darkness from the wise and the prudent. We must simplify our approach to Him. We must strip down to essentials (and they will be found to be blessedly few). We must put away all effort to impress, and come with the guileless candor of childhood. If we do this, without doubt God will quickly respond.

When religion has said its last word, there is little that we need other than God Himself. The evil habit of seeking God-and effectively prevents us from finding God in full revelation. In the and lies our great woe. If we omit the and, we shall soon find God, and in Him we shall find that for which we have all our lives been secretly longing.

We need not fear that in seeking God only we may narrow our lives or restrict the motions of our expanding hearts. The opposite is true. We can well afford to make God our All, to concentrate, to sacrifice the many for the One.

The author of the quaint old English classic *The Cloud of Unknowing* teaches us how to do this.

> Lift up thine heart unto God with a meek stirring of love; and mean Himself, and none of His goods. And thereto, look thee loath to think on aught but God Himself. So that nought work in thy wit, nor in thy will, but only God Himself. This is the work of the soul that most pleaseth God.

Again, he recommends that in prayer we practice a further stripping down of everything, even of our theology. "For it sufficeth enough, a naked intent direct unto God without any other cause than Himself." Yet underneath all his thinking lay the broad foundation of New Testament truth, for he explains that by "Himself" he means "God that made thee, and bought thee, and that graciously called thee, to thy degree." And he is all for simplicity:

> If we would have religion "lapped and folden in one word, for that thou shouldest have better hold thereupon, take thee but a little word of one syllable: for so it is better than of two, for even the shorter it is the better it accordeth with the work of the Spirit. And such a word is this word GOD or this word LOVE."

When the Lord divided Canaan among the tribes

of Israel, Levi received no share of the land. God said to him simply, "I am thy part and thine inheritance" (Numbers 18:20), and by those words made him richer than all his brethren, richer than all the kings and rajas who have ever lived in the world. And there is a spiritual principle here, a principle still valid for every priest of the Most High God.

The man who has God for his treasure has all things in One. Many ordinary treasures may be denied him, or if he is allowed to have them, the enjoyment of them will be so tempered that they will never be necessary to his happiness. Or if he must see them go, one after one, he will scarcely feel a sense of loss, for having the Source of all things he has in One all satisfaction, all pleasure, all delight. Whatever he may lose he has actually lost nothing, for he now has it all in One, and he has it purely, legitimately and forever.

O God, I have tasted Thy goodness, and it has both satisfied me and made me thirsty for more. I am painfully conscious of my need of further grace. I am ashamed of my lack of desire. O God, the Triune God, I want to want Thee; I long to be filled with longing; I thirst to be made more thirsty still. Show me Thy glory, I pray Thee, that so I may know Thee indeed. Begin in mercy a new work of love within me. Say to my soul, "Rise up, my love, my fair one, and come away." Then give me grace to rise and follow Thee up from this misty lowland where I have wandered so long. In Jesus' name. Amen.

Questions for Reflection
Following Hard after God

1. Tozer says that the "full knowledge of one personal-
    ity by another cannot be achieved in one encounter."
    In your day-to-day life, how often do you have en-
    counters with the person and personality of God?
    Are they vague or vibrant? What could you change
    or pray that God would change in your life to in-
    crease the frequency and vitality of these encoun-
    ters?

2. The impulse to pursue God originates with God.
    Has your response to that impulse been virtually
    nonexistent, sporadic and inconsistent, or steadily
    improving, with a growing longing to knowing Him
    better? Do you continually need others to encour-
    age you to pursue God, or has God been building
    that desire in your heart? Take the time to do an
    honest self-assessment, asking the Holy Spirit to
    search your heart.

3. How much of your seeking of God is done for you by
    teachers, books, Christian radio and TV programs?
    How much of your daily pursuit is spent listening
    to God and praying? Though teachers, books and
    media can be helpful, what makes private prayer
    and listening so important to your relationship with
    God?

4. On a scale of one to ten, rate the complexity of your daily life; compare that rating to your earlier assessment of your spiritual pursuit. How is a busy and complex life hostile to "the simplicity and purity of devotion to Christ" (2 Corinthians 11:3)? What is the solution to breaking free from the influence of complexity?

5. God purposely hides Himself from the wise and intelligent and reveals Himself to babes (Matthew 11:25). What must the individual believer do to become like a "babe"? "The man who has God for his treasure has all things in One." What should the believer's attitude be toward possessions, prestige, fame and more for his faith to blossom?

Chapter 2

God's Character

And they that know thy name will put their trust in thee. (Psalm 9:10)

In the messages that follow, we will consider that which is behind all things. There could be no more central or important theme. If you trace effect back to cause and that cause back to another cause and so on, back through the long dim corridors of the past until you come to the primordial atom out of which all things were made, you will find the One who made them—you'll find God.

Behind all previous matter, all life, all law, all space and all time, there is God. God gives to human life its only significance; there isn't any other apart from Him. If you take the concept of God out of the human mind, there is no other reason for being among the living. We are, as Tennyson said, like "sheep or goats/ That nourish a blind life within the brain."[1] And we might as well die as sheep unless we have God in our thoughts.

God is the source of all law and morality and goodness, the One that you must believe in before you can deny Him, the One who is the Word and the One that enables us to speak. I'm sure you will see immediately that in attempting a series of messages about the attributes of God, we run into that which is difficult above all things.

The famous preacher Sam Jones (who was a Billy Sunday before Billy Sunday's time) said that when the average preacher takes a text, it reminds him of an insect trying to carry a bale of cotton. And when I take my text and try to talk about God, I feel like that insect; only God can help me.

John Milton started to write a book on the fall of man and his restoration through Jesus Christ our Lord. He was to call his book *Paradise Lost*. But before he dared to write it, he prayed a prayer that I want to pray as well. He prayed to the Spirit, and he said, "And chiefly Thou O Spirit, that dost prefer/ Before all Temples th' upright heart and pure,/ Instruct me."[2]

I'd like to say, with no attempt at morbid humility, that without a pure heart and a surrendered mind, no man can preach worthily about God and no man can hear worthily. No man can hear these things unless God touches him and illuminates him. And so Milton said, "Instruct me, for Thou know'st; . . . What in me is dark/ Illumine, what is low raise and support;/ That to the highth of this great Argument/ I may assert th' Eternal Providence,/ And justifie the wayes of God to men."[3]

Who can speak about the attributes of God—His self-existence, His omniscience, His omnipotence, His transcendence and so on—who can do that and do it worthily? Who is capable of anything like that? I'm not. So I only have this one hope: As the poor little donkey rebuked the madness of the prophet and as the rooster crowed one night to arouse the apostle and bring him to repentance, so God may take me and use me. As Jesus rode into Jerusalem on the back of the little donkey, so I pray that He may be willing to ride out before the people on such an unworthy instrument as I.

It is utterly necessary that we know this God, this One that John wrote about, this One that the poet speaks about, this One that theology talks about and this One that we're sent to preach and teach about. It is absolutely, utterly and critically necessary that we know this One, for you see, man fell when he lost his right concept of God.

As long as man trusted God, everything was all right; human beings were healthy and holy (or at least innocent), and pure and good. But then the devil came along and threw a question mark into the mind of the woman: "And he said unto the woman, Yea, hath God said . . . ?" (Genesis 3:1). This was equivalent to sneaking around behind God's back and casting doubt on the goodness of God. And then began the progressive degeneration downward.

When the knowledge of God began to go out of the minds of men, we got into the fix that we're in now:

> Because that, when they knew God, they glorified him not as God, neither were thankful; but became vain in their imaginations, and their foolish heart was darkened. Professing themselves to be wise, they became fools, and changed the glory of the uncorruptible God into an image made like to corruptible man, and to birds, and fourfooted beasts, and creeping things. Wherefore God also gave them up to uncleanness through the lusts of their own hearts, to dishonour their own bodies between themselves: who changed the truth of God into a lie, and worshipped and served the creature more than the Creator, who is blessed for ever. Amen. For this cause God gave them up unto vile affections: for even their women did change the natural use into that which is against nature: and likewise also the men, leaving the natural use of the woman, burned in their lust one toward another; men with men working that which is unseemly, and receiving in themselves that recompense of their error which was meet. And even as they did not like to retain God in their knowledge, God gave them over to a reprobate mind, to do those things which are not convenient. (Romans 1:21–28)

That first chapter of Romans ends with a terrible charge of unrighteousness, fornication, wickedness, covetousness, maliciousness and all the long, black list of crimes and sins that man has been guilty of. All that came about because man lost his confidence in God. He didn't know God's character. He didn't know what kind of God God was. He got all mixed up about what God was like. Now the only way back is to have restored confidence in God. And the only way to have restored confidence in God is to have restored knowledge of God.

I began with the text, "And they that know thy name will put their trust in thee" (Psalm 9:10). The word *name* means character, plus reputation. "And they that know *what kind of God thou art* will put their trust in thee." We wonder why we don't have faith; the answer is, faith is confidence in the character of God, and if we don't know what kind of God God is, we can't have faith.

We read books about George Mueller and others and try to have faith. But we forget that faith is confidence in God's character. And because we are not aware of what kind of God God is, or what God is like, we cannot have faith. And so we struggle and wait and hope against hope. But faith doesn't come, because we do not know the character of God. "They that know what Thou art like will put their trust in Thee." It's automatic—it comes naturally when we know what kind of God God is.

I'm going to give you a report on the character of God, to tell you what God is like. And if you're listening with a worthy mind, you'll find faith will spring up. Ignorance and unbelief drag faith down, but a restored knowledge of God will bring faith up.

I don't suppose there is ever a time in the history of the world when we needed a restored knowledge of God more than we need it now. Bible-believing Christians have made great gains in the last forty years or so. We have more Bibles now than we've ever had—the Bible is a best seller. We have more Bible schools than we've ever had, ever in the history of the world. Millions of tons of gospel literature are being poured out all the time. There are more missions now than we know what to do with. And evangelism is riding very, very high at the present time. And more people go to church now, believe it or not, than ever went to church before.

Now all that has something in its favor, there's no doubt about it. But you know, a man can learn at the end of the year how his business stands by balancing off his losses with his gains. And while he may have some gains, if he has too many losses, he'll be out of business the next year.

Many of the gospel churches have made some gains over the last years, but we've also suffered one great central loss: our lofty concept of God. Christianity rises like an eagle and flies over the top of all the mountain peaks of all the religions of the world, chiefly because of her lofty concept of God, given to us in divine revelation and by the coming of the Son of God to take human flesh and dwell among us. Christianity, the great church, has for centuries lived on the character of God. She's preached God, she's prayed to God, she's declared God, she's honored God, she's elevated God, she's witnessed to God—the Triune God.

But in recent times there has been a loss suffered. We've suffered the loss of that high concept of God, and the concept of God handled by the average gospel church now is so low as to be unworthy of God and a disgrace to the church. It is by neglect, degenerate error and spiritual blindness that some are saying God is their "pardner" or "the man upstairs." One Christian college put out a booklet called *Christ Is My Quarterback*—He always calls the right play. And a certain businessman was quoted as saying, "God's a good fellow and I like Him."

There isn't a Muslim alive in the world who would stoop to calling God a "good fellow." There isn't a Jew, at least no Jew who believes in his religion, that would ever dare to refer that way to the great Yahweh, the One with the incommunicable name. They talk about God respectfully and reverently. But in the gospel churches, God is a "quarterback" and a "good fellow."

I sometimes feel like walking out on a lot that passes for Christianity. They talk about prayer as "going into a huddle with God," as if God is the coach or the quarterback or something; they all gather around, God gives the signal and away they go. What preposterous abomination! When the Romans sacrificed a sow on the altar in Jerusalem, they didn't commit anything more frightful than when we drag the holy, holy, holy God down and turn Him into a cheap Santa Claus that we can use to get what we want.

Christianity has lost its dignity. And we'll never get it back unless we know the dignified holy God, who rides on the wings of the wind and makes the clouds His chariots. We have lost the concept of majesty and the art of worship. I got a letter from my good friend Stacy Woods, who was until recently head of InterVarsity. And he said this in the closing lines of his letter: "The church is getting away from worship. I wonder if it is because we are getting away from God." I think he's right, and I believe that is the answer.

And then our religion has lost its inwardness. For Christianity, if it's anything, is an inward religion. Jesus said that we are to worship in spirit and in truth (see John 4:24). And yet we've lost it because we have lost the concept of deity that makes it possible. Even though we've hung onto our Scofield Bible and still believe in the seven main doctrines of the fundamental faith, we've lost the awe, the wonder, the fear and the delight. Why? Because we've lost God, or at least we've lost our high and lofty concept of God—the only concept of God that

He honors.

And so the gains we have made have all been external: Bibles and Bible schools; books and magazines and radio messages; missions and evangelism; numbers and new churches. And the losses we've suffered have all been internal: the loss of dignity and worship and majesty, of inwardness, of God's presence, of fear and spiritual delight.

If we have lost only that which is inward and gained only that which is outward, I wonder if we've gained anything at all. I wonder if we are not now in a bad state. I believe we are. I believe our gospel churches, our Christianity, is thin and anemic, without thoughtful content, frivolous in tone and worldly in spirit.

And I believe that we are desperately in need of a reformation that will bring the church back.

I quit using the word revival because we need more than a revival. When the great Welsh revival came to the little country of Wales around the turn of the century, the Holy Ghost had something to work with. The people believed in God and their concept of God was lofty. But because the church has lost her lofty concept of God and no longer knows what God is like, her religion is thin and anemic, frivolous and worldly and cheap.

Compare the preaching of the church today with that of the Hebrew prophets, or even of men like Charles Finney—if you dare to do it. How serious these men of God were! They were men of heaven come to earth to speak to men. As Moses came down from the mount with his face shining to speak to men, so the prophets and preachers down through the years went out. Serious-minded men they were, solemn men, lofty in tone and full of substance of thought and theology.

But today the preaching to a large extent is cheap, frivolous, coarse, shallow and entertaining. We in the gospel churches think that we've got to entertain the people or they won't come back. We have lost the seriousness out of our preaching and have become silly. We've lost the solemnity and have become fearless, we've lost the loftiness and have become coarse and shallow. We've lost the substance and have become entertainers. This is a tragic and terrible thing.

Compare the Christian reading matter and you'll know that we're in pretty much the same situation. The Germans, the Scots, the Irish, the Welsh, the English, the Americans and the Canadians all have a common Protestant heritage. And what did they read, these Protestant forebears of yours and mine? Well, they read Doddridge's *The Rise and Progress of Religion in the Soul*. They read Taylor's *Holy Living and Dying*. They read Bunyan's *Pilgrim's Progress* and *Holy War*. They read Milton's *Paradise Lost*. They read the sermons of John Flavel.

And I blush today to think about the religious fodder that is now being handed out to children. There was a day when they sat around as the fire crackled in the hearth and listened to a serious but kindly old grandfather read *Pilgrim's Progress*, and the young Canadian and the young American grew up knowing all about Mr. Facing-Both-Ways and all the rest of that gang. And now we read cheap junk that ought to be shoveled out and gotten rid of.

Then I think about the songs that are sung now in so many places. Ah, the roster of the sweet singers! There's Watts, who wrote "Oh, God, Our Help in Ages Past," and Zinzendorf, who wrote so many great hymns. And then there was Wesley, who's written so many. There was Newton and there was Cooper, who wrote "There Is a Fountain Filled with Blood," and Montgomery and the two Bernards— Bernard of Cluny and Bernard of Clairvaux. There was Paul Gerhardt and Tersteegen, there was Luther and Kelly, Addison and Toplady, Senic and Doddridge, Tate and Brady and the Scottish Psalter. And there was a company of others that weren't as big as these great stars, but taken together they made a Milky Way that circled the Protestant sky.

I have an old Methodist hymnal that rolled off the press 111 years ago and I found forty-nine hymns on the attributes of God in it. I have heard it said that we shouldn't sing hymns with so much theology because peoples' minds are different now. We think differently now. Did you know that those Methodist hymns were sung mostly by uneducated people? They were farmers and sheepherders and cattle ranchers, coal miners and blacksmiths, carpenters and cotton pickers—plain people all over this continent. They sang those songs. There are more than 1,100 hymns in that hymnbook of mine, and there isn't a cheap one in the whole bunch.

And nowadays, I won't even talk about some of the terrible junk that we sing. They have a little one that is sung to the tune of "There'll Be a Hot Time in the Old Town Tonight," which goes like this:

One, two, three, the devil's after me,
Four, five, six, he's always throwing bricks,
Seven, eight, nine, he misses every time,
Hallelujah, Hallelujah. Amen.

And the dear saints of God sing that now! Our fathers sang "O God, Our Help in Ages Past," and we sing junk.

This tragic and frightening decline in the spiritual state of the churches has come about as a result of our forgetting what kind of God God is.

We have lost the vision of the Majesty on high. I have been reading in the book of Ezekiel during the last weeks, reading slowly and rereading, and I've just come to that terrible, frightening, awful passage where the *Shekinah*, the shining presence of God, lifts up from between the wings of the cherubim, goes to the altar, lifts up from the altar, goes to the door and there is the sound of the whirring of wings (see Ezekiel 10:4–5). And then the presence of God goes from the door to the outer court (see 10:18–19) and from the outer court to the mountain (see 11:23) and from the mountain into the glory.

And it has never been back, except as it was incarnated in Jesus Christ when He walked among us. But the *Shekinah* glory that had followed Israel about all those years, that shone over the camp, was gone. God couldn't take it any longer, so He pulled out His Majesty, His *Shekinah* glory, and left the temple. And I wonder how many gospel churches, by their frivolousness, shallowness, coarseness and worldliness, have grieved the Holy Ghost until He's withdrawn in hurt silence. We must see God again; we must feel God again; we must know God again; we must hear God again. Nothing less than this will save us.

I'm hoping that you will be prayerful and that you'll be worthy to hear this, and that I'll be worthy to speak about God—the Triune God, the Father, Son and Holy Ghost—what He's like. If we can restore again knowledge of God to men, we can help in some small way to bring about a reformation that will restore God again to men. I want to close with these words of Frederick Faber:

> Full of glory, full of wonders,
> Majesty Divine!
> Mid thine everlasting thunders
> How thy lightnings shine.
> Shoreless Ocean! who shall sound Thee?
> Thine own eternity is round Thee,
> Majesty Divine![4]

One hour with the majesty of God would be worth more to you now and in eternity than all the preachers—including myself—that ever stood up to open their Bible. I want a vision of the majesty of God—not as that song says, "one transient gleam"—no, I don't want anything transient, I want the gleam of majesty and wonder to be permanent! I want to live where the face of God shines every day. No child says, "Mother, let me see your face transiently." The child wants to be where any minute of the hour he can look up and see his mother's face.

> Timeless, spaceless, single, lonely,
> Yet sublimely Three,
> Thou art grandly, always, only
> God in Unity!
> Lone in grandeur, lone in glory,
> Who shall tell thy wondrous story,
> Awful Trinity?
> Splendours upon splendours beaming
> Change and intertwine;
> Glories over glories streaming
> All translucent shine!
> Blessings, praises, adorations
> Greet thee from the trembling nations
> Majesty Divine![5]

This is the day of the common man—and we have not only all become common, but we've dragged God down to our mediocre level. What we need so desperately is an elevated concept of God.

Maybe by faithful preaching and prayer, and by the Holy Ghost, we can see the "splendours upon splendours beaming/ Change and intertwine." Maybe we can see "Glories over glories streaming/ All translucent shine!" To God we can give "blessings, praises, adorations" that "Greet thee from the trembling nations/ Majesty Divine!"

Questions for Reflection
God's Character

1. "And they that know thy name will put their trust in thee" (Psalm 9:10, KJV). The names of God reflect the character of God, both in simplicity and in great depth. Tozer notes that it is no "wonder why we don't have faith; the answer is, faith is confidence in the character of God, and if we don't know what kind of God God is, we can't have faith." Try a thirty-day experiment of reflecting and meditating on a different name of God every day. What other steps of action could you take to expand your understanding of God's character and eventually impact your faith?

2. Tozer says faith "is automatic—it comes naturally when we know what kind of God God is." Reflect on a recent situation where your faith was tested and you won the battle. What aspects of God's character were the springboards for your faith response in that situation?

3. "Ignorance and unbelief drag faith down, but a restored knowledge of God will bring faith up." What are some specific ways we can fight ignorance and unbelief in our daily life, gain a revived perspective of God and His character and grow in our faith?

4. "Christianity has lost its dignity," Tozer declares. "And we'll never get it back unless we know the dignified holy God, who rides on the wings of the wind and makes the clouds His chariots." What does Tozer mean by dignity? How do we approach God with the dignity He deserves? Read Psalm 104 and meditate upon the majesty and dignity of God.

5. Tozer notes that our gains in religion have all been external and "the losses we've suffered have all been internal: the loss of dignity and worship and majesty, of inwardness, of God's presence, of fear and spiritual delight." Tozer was speaking to a previous generation, but many of his observations apply as well to the church today. Change can only come, of course, on an individual level. Spend some time in self-examination: Have your gains been more external than internal? Have you experienced a loss of inward communion with the Lord? What must be done immediately and long-term to flip the focus inward and allow the outward to come in God's time? Spend some time in prayer before the throne of God, confessing any lukewarmness of heart, and ask God to strengthen your inner life of faith.

Chapter 3

Apprehending God

O taste and see. (Psalm 34:8)

Canon Holmes, of India, more than twenty-five years ago called attention to the inferential character of the average man's faith in God. To most people God is an inference, not a reality. He is a deduction from evidence that they consider adequate, but He remains personally unknown to the individual. "He *must* be," they say, "therefore we believe He is." Others do not go even so far as this; they know of Him only by hearsay. They have never bothered to think the matter out for themselves, but have heard about Him from others, and have put belief in Him into the back of their minds along with various odds and ends that make up their total

31

creed. To many others, God is but an ideal, another name for goodness or beauty or truth; or He is law or life or the creative impulse back of the phenomena of existence.

These notions about God are many and varied, but they who hold them have one thing in common: They do not know God in personal experience. The possibility of intimate acquaintance with Him has not entered their minds. While admitting His existence, they do not think of Him as being knowable in the sense that we know things or people.

Christians, to be sure, go further than this, at least in theory. Their creed requires them to believe in the personality of God, and they have been taught to pray, "Our Father which art in heaven" (Luke 11:2). Now personality and fatherhood carry with them the idea of the possibility of personal acquaintance. This is admitted, I say, in theory, but for millions of Christians, nevertheless, God is no more real than He is to the non-Christian. They go through life trying to love an ideal and be loyal to a mere principle.

Against all this cloudy vagueness stands the clear scriptural doctrine that God can be known in personal experience. A loving personality dominates the Bible, walking among the trees of the garden and breathing fragrance over every scene. Always a living person is present, speaking, pleading, loving, working and manifesting Himself whenever and wherever His people have the receptivity necessary to receive the manifestation.

The Bible assumes as a self-evident fact that men can know God with at least the same degree of immediacy as they know any other person or thing that comes within the field of their experience. The same terms are used to express the knowledge of God as are used to express knowledge of physical things. "O *taste* and see that the LORD is good" (Psalm 34:8, emphasis added). "All thy garments *smell* of myrrh, and aloes, and cassia, out of the ivory palaces" (45:8). "My sheep *hear* my voice" (John 10:27, emphasis added). "Blessed are the pure in heart: for they shall *see* God" (Matthew 5:8, emphasis added). These are but four of countless such passages from the Word of God. And more important than any proof text is the fact that the whole import of Scripture is toward this belief.

What can all this mean except that we have in our hearts organs by means of which we can know God as certainly as we know material things through our familiar five senses? We apprehend the physical world by exercising the faculties given us for that purpose, and we possess spiritual faculties by means of which we can know God and the spiritual world if we will obey the Spirit's urge and begin to use them.

That a saving work must first be done in the heart is taken for granted here. The spiritual faculties of the unregenerate man lie asleep in his nature, unused, and for every purpose dead. That is the stroke that has fallen upon us by sin. They may be quickened to active life again by the operation of the Holy Spirit in regeneration. That is one of the immeasurable benefits that comes to us through Christ's atoning work on the cross.

But why do the very ransomed children of God themselves know so little of that habitual, conscious communion with God that Scripture offers? The answer is because of our chronic unbelief. Faith enables our spiritual sense to function. Where faith is defective, the result will be inward insensibility and numbness toward spiritual things. This is the condition of vast numbers of Christians today. No proof is necessary to support that statement. We have but to converse with the first Christian we meet or enter the first church we open to acquire all the proof we need.

A spiritual kingdom lies all about us, enclosing us, embracing us, altogether within reach of our inner selves, waiting for us to recognize it. God Himself is here awaiting our response to His presence. This eternal world will come alive to us the moment we begin to reckon upon its reality.

I have just now used two words that demand definition. Or if definition is impossible, I must at least make clear what I mean when I use them. They are *reckon* and *reality*.

What do I mean by *reality*? I mean that which has existence apart from any idea any mind may have of it, and which would exist if there were no mind anywhere to entertain a thought of it. That which is real has being in itself. It does not depend upon the observer for its validity.

I am aware that there are those who love to poke fun at the plain man's idea of reality. They are the idealists who spin endless proofs that nothing is real outside of the mind. They are the relativists who like to show that there are no fixed points in the universe from which we can measure anything. They smile down upon us from their lofty intellectual peaks and settle us to their own satisfaction by fastening upon us the reproachful term "absolutist." The Christian is not put out of countenance by this show of contempt. He can smile right back at them, for he knows that there is only One who is Absolute; that is God. But he knows also that the Absolute One has made this world for man's use, and while there is nothing fixed or real in the last meaning of the words (the meaning as applied to God), for every purpose of human life, we are permitted to act as if there were. And every man does act thus except the mentally sick. These unfortunates also have trouble with reality, but they are consistent; they insist upon living in accordance with their ideas of things. They are honest, and it is their very honesty that constitutes them a social problem.

The idealists and relativists are not mentally sick. They prove their soundness by living their lives according to the very notions of reality that they in theory repudiate and by counting upon the very fixed points that they prove are not there. They could earn a lot more respect for their notions if they were willing to live by them; but this they are careful not to do. Their ideas are brain-deep, not life-deep. Wherever life touches them, they repudiate their theories and live like other men.

The Christian is too sincere to play with ideas for their own sake. He takes no pleasure in the mere spinning of gossamer webs for display. All his beliefs are practical. They are geared into his life. By them he lives or dies, stands or falls for this world and for all time to come. From the insincere man he turns away.

The sincere, plain man knows that the world is real. He finds it here when he wakes to consciousness, and he knows that he did not think it into being. It was here waiting for him when he came, and he knows that when he prepares to leave this earthly scene, it will be here still to bid him good-bye as he departs. By the deep wisdom of life, he is wiser than a thousand men who doubt. He stands upon the earth and feels the wind and rain in his face, and he knows that they are real. He sees the sun by day and the stars by night. He sees the hot lightning play out of the dark thundercloud. He hears the sounds of nature and the cries of human joy and pain. These he knows are real. He lies down on the cool earth at night and has no fear that it will prove illusory or fail him while he sleeps. In the morning the firm ground will be under him, the blue sky above him and the rocks and trees around him as when he closed his eyes the night before. So he lives and rejoices in a world of reality.

With his five senses, he engages this real world. All things necessary to his physical existence he apprehends by the faculties with which he has been equipped by the God who created him and placed him in such a world as this.

Now by our definition also God is real. He is real in the absolute and final sense that nothing else is. All other reality is contingent upon His. The great Reality is God, the Author of that lower and dependent reality that makes up the sum of created things, including ourselves. God has objective existence independent of and apart from any notions that we may have concerning Him. The worshipping heart does not create its Object. It finds Him here when it wakes from its mortal slumber in the morning of its regeneration.

Another word that must be cleared up is *reckon*. This does not mean to visualize or imagine. Imagination is not faith. The two are not only different from, but stand in sharp opposition to, each other. Imagination projects unreal images out of the mind and seeks to attach reality to them. Faith creates nothing; it simply reckons upon that which is already there.

God and the spiritual world are real. We can reckon upon them with as much assurance as we reckon upon the familiar world around us. Spiritual things are there (or rather we should say here) inviting our attention and challenging our trust.

Our trouble is that we have established bad thought habits. We habitually think of the visible world as real and doubt the reality of any other. We do not deny the existence of the spiritual world, but we doubt that it is real in the accepted meaning of the word.

The world of sense intrudes upon our attention day and night for the whole of our lifetime. It is clamorous, insistent and self-demonstrating. It does not appeal to our faith; it is here, assaulting our five senses, demanding to be accepted as real and final. But sin has so clouded the lenses of our hearts that we cannot see that other reality, the City of God, shining around us. The world of sense triumphs. The visible becomes the enemy of the invisible, the temporal of the eternal. That is the curse inherited by every member of Adam's tragic race.

At the root of the Christian life lies belief in the invisible. The object of the Christian's faith is unseen reality.

Our uncorrected thinking, influenced by the blindness of our natural hearts and the intrusive ubiquity of visible things, tends to draw a contrast between the spiritual and the real—but actually no such contrast exists. The antithesis lies elsewhere—between the real and the imaginary, between the spiritual and the material, between the temporal and the eternal; but between the spiritual and the real, never. The spiritual is real.

If we would rise into that region of light and power plainly beckoning us through the Scriptures of truth, we must break the evil habit of ignoring the spiritual. We must shift our interest from the seen to the unseen. For the great unseen Reality is God. "He that cometh to God must believe that he is, and that he is a rewarder of them that diligently seek him" (Hebrews 11:6). This is basic in the life of faith. From there we can rise to unlimited heights. "Ye believe in God," said our Lord Jesus Christ, "believe also in me" (John 14:1). Without the first there can be no second.

If we truly want to follow God, we must seek to be otherworldly. This I say knowing well that word has been used with scorn by the sons of this world and applied to the Christian as a badge of reproach. So be it. Every man must choose his world. If we who follow Christ, with all the facts before us and knowing what we are about, deliberately choose the kingdom of God as our sphere of interest, I see no reason why anyone should object. If we lose by it, the loss is our own; if we gain, we rob no one by so doing. The "other world," which is the object of this world's disdain and the subject of the drunkard's mocking song, is our carefully chosen goal and the object of our holiest longing.

But we must avoid the common fault of pushing the "other world" into the future. It is not future, but present. It parallels our familiar physical world, and the doors between the two worlds are open. "Ye are come," says the writer to the Hebrews (and the tense is plainly present),

> unto mount Sion, and unto the city of the living God, the heavenly Jerusalem, and to an innumerable company of angels, to the general assembly and church of the firstborn, which are written in heaven, and to God the Judge of all, and to the spirits of just men made perfect, and to Jesus the mediator of the new covenant, and to the blood of sprinkling, that speaketh better things than that of Abel. (Hebrews 12:22–24)

All these things are contrasted with "the mount that might be touched" (12:18) and "the sound of a trumpet, and the voice of words" (12:19) that might be heard. May we not safely conclude that, as the realities of Mount Sinai were apprehended by the senses, so the realities of Mount Zion are to be grasped by the soul? And this not by any trick of the imagination but in downright actuality. The soul has eyes with which to see and ears with which to hear. Feeble they may be from long disuse, but by the life-giving touch of Christ, they are now alive and capable of sharpest sight and most sensitive hearing.

As we begin to focus upon God, the things of the spirit will take shape before our inner eyes. Obedience to the word of Christ will bring an inward revelation of the Godhead (see John 14:21–23). It will give acute perception enabling us to see God even as is promised to the pure in heart. A new God-consciousness will seize upon us and we shall begin to taste and hear and inwardly feel God, who is our life and our all. There will be seen the constant shining of "the true Light, which lighteth every man that cometh into the world" (John 1:9). More and more, as our faculties grow sharper and more sure, God will become to us the great All, and His presence the glory and wonder of our lives.

O God, quicken to life every power within me, that I may lay hold on eternal things. Open my eyes that I may see; give me acute spiritual perception; enable me to taste Thee and know that Thou art good. Make heaven more real to me than any earthly thing has ever been. Amen.

Questions for Reflection
Apprehending God

1. For millions of Christians, God is no more real than He is to the non-Christian. As Tozer notes, this Christian goes through life trying to love an ideal and to be loyal to a principle. It is a life devoid of power, divine joy, the taste of God's goodness and any personal experience with God. What causes this lack of habitual, conscious communion with the Father? How can this be corrected?

2. "Faith enables our spiritual sense to function," Tozer says, and goes on to mention numbness and insensibility toward spiritual things as telltale signs of a defective faith. List some other signs and ask yourself if you have been guilty of any of them in the past six months.

3. The greatest Reality is God; all other realities are contingent upon Him. How does one adopt and stay faithful to this truth in such a way that it makes a difference every day?

4. As believers "we must break the evil habit of ignor-
    ing the spiritual." Tozer calls us to shift our inter-
    est from the seen to the great unseen Reality, God
    Himself. What are some small steps that can aid this
    shift? Why must we fight this shift every day in the
    power of the Holy Spirit?

5. In this chapter, Tozer is encouraging believers to de-
    velop a new God-consciousness. Reflect on how sin,
    disobedience, lack of prayer, lack of love for others
    and lack of personal study in God's Word affect this
    God-consciousness.

Chapter 4

The Eternal Continuum

"As I was with Moses, so I will be with thee."
(Joshua 1:5)

The unconditioned priority of God in His universe is a truth celebrated both in the Old Testament and in the New. The prophet Habakkuk sang it in ecstatic language, "Art thou not from everlasting, O LORD my God, mine Holy One?" (1:12). The Apostle John set it forth in careful words deep with meaning, "In the beginning was the Word, and the Word was with God, and the Word was God. The same was in the beginning with God. All things were made by him; and without him was not any thing made that was made" (1:1–3).

This truth is so necessary to right thoughts about

God and ourselves that it can hardly be too strongly emphasized. It is a truth known to everyone, a kind of common property of all religious persons, but for the very reason that it is so common it now has but little meaning for any of us. It has suffered the fate of which Coleridge writes:

> Truths, of all others the most awful and interesting, are too often considered as so true that they lose all the power of truth and lie bedridden in the dormitory of the soul, side by side with the most despised and exploded errors.

The divine priority is one of those bedridden truths. I desire to do what I can to rescue it "from the neglect caused by the very circumstance of its universal admission." Neglected Christian truths can be revitalized only when by prayer and long meditation we isolate them from the mass of hazy ideas with which our minds are filled and hold them steadily and determinedly in the focus of the mind's attention.

For all things God is the great Antecedent. Because He is, we are and everything else is. He is that "dread, unbeginning One," self-caused, self-contained and self-sufficient. Faber saw this when he wrote his great hymn in celebration of God's eternity.

> Thou hast no youth, great God,
> An Unbeginning End Thou art;

Thy glory in itself abode,
And still abides in its own tranquil heart:
No age can heap its outward years on Thee:
Dear God! Thou art Thyself Thine own eternity.

Do not skip this as merely another poem. The difference between a great Christian life and any other kind lies in the quality of our religious concepts, and the ideas expressed in these six lines can be like rungs on Jacob's ladder leading upward to a sounder and more satisfying idea of God.

We cannot think rightly of God until we begin to think of Him as always being *there*, and *there first*. Joshua had this to learn. He had been so long the servant of God's servant Moses, and had with such assurance received God's word at his mouth, that Moses and the God of Moses had become blended in his thinking, so blended that he could hardly separate the two thoughts; by association they always appeared together in his mind. Now Moses is dead, and lest the young Joshua be struck down with despair, God spoke to assure him, "As I was with Moses, so I will be with thee" (Joshua 1:5; 3:7). Nothing had changed, and nothing had been lost. Nothing of God dies when a man of God dies.

"As I was—so I will be." Only God could say this. Only the Eternal One could stand in the timeless I AM and say, "I was" and "I will be."

Here we acknowledge (and there is fear and wonder in the thought) the essential unity of God's nature, the timeless persistence of His changeless being throughout eternity and time. Here we begin to see and feel the eternal continuum. Begin where we will, God is there first. He is Alpha and Omega, the beginning and the ending, which was, and which is and which is to come, the Almighty. If we grope back to the farthest limits of thought where imagination touches the pre-creation void, we shall find God there. In one unified present glance He comprehends all things from everlasting, and the flutter of a seraph's wing a thousand ages hence is seen by Him now without moving His eyes.

Once I should have considered such thoughts to be mere metaphysical bric-a-brac without practical meaning for anyone in a world such as this. Now I recognize them as sound and easy-to-grasp truths with unlimited potential for good. Failure to get a right viewpoint in the beginning of our Christian lives may result in weakness and sterility for the rest of our days. May not the inadequacy of much of our spiritual experience be traced back to our habit of skipping through the corridors of the kingdom like children through the marketplace, chattering about everything but pausing to learn the true value of nothing?

In my creature impatience I am often caused to wish that there were some way to bring modern Christians into a deeper spiritual life painlessly by short, easy lessons; but such wishes are vain. No shortcut exists. God has not bowed to our nervous haste nor embraced the methods of our machine age. It is well that we accept the hard truth now: *The man who would know God must give time to Him*. He must count no time wasted that is spent in the cultivation of His acquaintance. He must give himself to meditation and prayer hours on end. So did the saints of old, the glorious company of the apostles, the goodly fellowship of the prophets and the believing members of the holy church in all generations. And so must we if we would follow in their train.

We would think of God, then, as maintaining the unity of His uncreated being throughout all His works and His years, as ever saying not only, "I did," and "I will do," but also "I do," and "I am doing."

A robust faith requires that we grasp this truth firmly, yet we know how seldom such a thought enters our minds. We habitually stand in our *now* and look back by faith to see the past filled with God. We look forward and see Him inhabiting our future; but our *now* is uninhabited except for ourselves. Thus we are guilty of a kind of temporary atheism, which leaves us alone in the universe while, for the time, God is not. We talk of Him much and loudly, but we secretly think of Him as being absent, and we think of ourselves as inhabiting a parenthetic interval between the God who was and the God who will be. And we are lonely with an ancient and cosmic loneliness. We are each like a little child lost in a crowded market, who has strayed but a few feet from its mother, yet because she cannot be seen, the child is inconsolable. So we try by every method devised by religion to relieve our fears and heal our hidden sadness; but with all our efforts we remain unhappy still, with the settled despair of men alone in a vast and deserted universe.

But for all our fears we are not alone. Our trouble is that we *think* of ourselves as being alone. Let us correct the error by thinking of ourselves as standing by the bank of a full flowing river; then let us think of that river as being none else but God Himself. We glance to our left and see the river coming full out of our past; we look to the right and see it flowing on into our future. *But we see also that it is flowing through our present.* And in our today it is the same as it was in our yesterday, not less than, nor different from, but the very same river, one unbroken continuum, undiminished, active and strong as it moves sovereignly on into our tomorrow.

Wherever faith has been original, wherever it has proved itself to be real, it has invariably had upon it a sense of the *present God*. The holy Scriptures possess in marked degree this feeling of actual encounter with a real person. The men and women of the Bible talked with God. They spoke to Him and heard Him speak in words they could understand. With Him they held person-to-person interaction, and a sense of shining reality is upon their words and deeds.

The world's own prophets, the unbelieving psychologists (those eyeless seekers who seek for a light that is not God's light), have been forced to recognize at the bottom of religious experience this sense of *something there*. But better far is the sense of *Someone there*. It was this that filled with abiding wonder the first members of the church of Christ. The solemn delight which those early disciples knew sprang straight from the conviction that there was One in the midst of them. They knew that the Majesty in the heavens was confronting them on earth: They were in the very Presence of God. And the power of that conviction to arrest attention and hold it for a lifetime, to elevate, to transform, to fill with uncontrollable moral happiness, to send men singing to prison and to death, has been one of the wonders of history and a marvel of the world.

Our fathers have told us and our own hearts confirm how wonderful is this sense of Someone there. It makes religion invulnerable to critical attack. It secures the mind against collapse under the battering of the enemy. They who worship the God who is present may ignore the objections of unbelieving men. Their experience is self-verifying and needs neither defense nor proof. What they see and hear overwhelms their doubts and confirms their assurance beyond the power of argument to destroy.

Some who desire to be teachers of the Word, but who understand neither what they say, nor whereof they affirm, insist upon "naked" faith as the only way to know spiritual things. By this they mean a conviction of the trustworthiness of the Word of God (a conviction, it may be noted, that the devils share with them).

But the man who has been taught even slightly by the Spirit of Truth will rebel at this perversion. His language will be, "I have heard Him and observed Him. What have I to do any more with idols?" For he cannot love a God who is no more than a deduction from a text. He will crave to know God with a vital awareness that goes beyond words and to live in the intimacy of personal communion.

> To seek our divinity merely in books and writings is to *seek the living among the dead;* we do but in vain many times seek God in these, where his truth too often is not so much enshrined as entombed . . . he is best discerned by an intellectual touch of him . . . we must see with our eyes, and hear with our ears, and our hands must handle of the word of Life. [John Smith of Cambridge]

Nothing can take the place of the *touch* of God in the soul and the sense of Someone there. Real faith, indeed, brings such realization, for real faith is never the operation of reason upon texts. Where true faith is, the knowledge of God will be given as a fact of consciousness altogether apart from the conclusions of logic.

Were a man to awaken in the pitch dark at midnight and hear someone moving about in his room and know that the unseen presence was a loved member of his family who had every right to be there, his heart might be filled with a sense of quiet pleasure; but should he have reason to believe that an intruder had entered, perhaps to rob or to kill, he would lie in terror and stare at the darkness not knowing from which direction the expected blow might come. But *the difference between experience and no experience would be that acute sense of someone there.* Is it not true that for most of us who call ourselves Christians, there is no real experience? We have substituted theological ideas for an arresting encounter; we are full of religious notions, but our great weakness is that for our hearts there is no one there.

Whatever else it embraces, true Christian experience must always include a genuine encounter with God. Without this, religion is but a shadow, a reflection of reality, a cheap copy of an original once enjoyed by someone else of whom we have heard. It cannot but be a major tragedy in the life of any man to live in a church from childhood to old age and know nothing more real than some synthetic god compounded of theology and logic, but having no eyes to see, no ears to hear and no heart to love.

The spiritual giants of old were men who at some time became acutely conscious of the real Presence of God and maintained that consciousness for the rest of their lives. The first encounter may have been one of terror, as when a "horror of great darkness" (Genesis 15:12) fell upon Abram, or as when Moses at the bush hid his face because he was afraid to look upon God (see Exodus 3:1–6). Usually this fear soon lost its content of terror and changed after a while to delightsome awe, to level off finally into a reverent sense of complete nearness to God. The essential point is, *they experienced God.* How otherwise can the saints and prophets be explained? How otherwise can we account for the amazing power for good they have exercised over countless generations? Is it not that they walked in conscious communion with the real Presence and addressed their prayers to God with the artless conviction that they were addressing Someone actually there?

Without doubt we have suffered the loss of many spiritual treasures because we have let slip the simple truth that the miracle of the perpetuation of life is in God. God did not create life and toss it from Him like some petulant artist disappointed with his work. All life is in Him and out of Him, flowing from Him and returning to Him again, a moving indivisible sea of which He is the Fountainhead. That eternal life that was with the Father is now the possession of believing men, and that life is not God's gift only, but His very self.

Redemption is not a strange work that God for a moment turned aside to do; rather, it is His same work performed in a new field, the field of human catastrophe. The regeneration of a believing soul is but a recapitulation of all His work done from the moment of creation. It is hard to miss the parallel between generation as described in the Old Testament and regeneration as described in the New. How, for instance, could the condition of a lost soul better be described than by the words, "without form, and void" with darkness "upon the face of the deep" (Genesis 1:2)? And how could the strong yearnings of God's heart over that lost soul be more perfectly expressed than by saying that "the spirit of God moved upon the face of the waters" (1:2)? And from what source could light come to that sin-shrouded soul had God not said, "Let there be light" (1:3)? At His word the light breaks and the lost man arises to drink of eternal life and follow the Light of the world. As order and fruitfulness came next to that ancient creation, so moral order and spiritual fruit follow next in human experience. And we know that God is the same and His years fail not (see Hebrews 1:12). He will always act like Himself wherever He is found at work and whatever work He is doing.

We need to seek deliverance from our vain and weakening wish to go back and recover the past. We should seek to be cleansed from the childish notion that to have lived in Abram's day, or in Paul's, would have been better than to live today. With God, Abram's day and this day are the same. By one single impulse of life He created all days and all times, so that the life of the first day and the life of the remotest future day are united in Him. We may well sing again (and believe) the truth our fathers sang:

> Eternity with all its years,
>> Stands present in Thy view;
> To Thee there's nothing old appears;
>> Great God, there's nothing new.

In saving men God is but doing again (or rather continuing to do) the same creative work as at the beginning of the world. To Him each ransomed soul is a world wherein He performs again His pleasant work as of old.

We who experience God in this day may rejoice that we have in Him all that Abraham or David or Paul could have; indeed the very angels before the throne can have no more than we, for they can have no more God and can want nothing apart from Him. And all that He is and all that He has done is for us and for all who share the common salvation. With full consciousness of our own demerit, we may yet take our place in the love of God, and the poorest and weakest of us may without offense claim for ourselves all the riches of the Godhead in mercy given. I have every right to claim all for myself, knowing that an infinite God can give all of Himself to each of His children. He does not distribute Himself that each may have a part, but to each one He gives all of Himself as fully as if there were no others.

What a difference it makes when we cease being general (a dodge, incidentally, for pseudo-humility and unbelief) and become pointed and personal in our approach to God. Then we shall not fear the personal pronoun but shall with the friends of God relate it to the One who gave it and claim each one for himself the person and work of the Triune God. Then we shall see that all that God did was for each of us. Then we can sing:

> For me Thou didst cover Thyself with light as with a garment and stretch out the heavens like a curtain and lay the foundations of the earth. For me Thou didst appoint the moon for seasons and the sun knoweth his going down. For me Thou didst make every beast of the earth after his kind and every herb-bearing seed and every tree in which is the fruit of a tree. For me prophet wrote and psalmist sang. For me holy men spake as they were moved by the Holy Ghost.

> For me Christ died, and the redemptive benefits of that death are by the miracle of His present life perpetuated forever, as efficacious now as on the day He bowed His head and gave up the ghost. And when He arose the third day it was for me; and when He poured out upon the disciples the promised Holy Spirit it was that He might continue in me the work He had been doing for me since the morning of the creation.

Questions for Reflection
The Eternal Continuum

1. "For all things God is the Great Antecedent. Because He is, we are and everything else is. He is that 'dread, unbeginning One,' self-caused, self-contained, and self-sufficient." This may be the hardest thought of all for our natural egotistic minds to grasp: God does not need our help, yet we desperately need His. He is self-sufficient, and we are not. Why is this principle so critical to our understanding and so foundational to the progress of our faith?

2. Tozer warns us not to look for shortcuts to a deeper spiritual life: "God has not bowed to our nervous haste nor embraced the methods of our machine age. It is well that we accept the hard truth now: The man who would know God must give time to Him. He must count no time wasted that is spent in the cultivation of His acquaintance." What makes the shortcut mentality so injurious to a life of faith? How does one cultivate an acquaintance with the living God in a fast-paced culture? What must our motivation be for this pursuit?

3. A robust faith in God not only understands what God did (past) and what God will do (future) but also what He does and is doing (present). We believers today tend to "habitually stand in our *now* and

look back by faith to see the past filled with God. We look forward and see Him inhabiting our future; but our *now* is uninhabited except for ourselves. Thus we are guilty of a kind of temporary atheism which leaves us alone in the universe, while for the time, God is not." Why is this perspective of life so destructive to our faith? How can we assess whether or not we are caught up in this vortex of "temporary atheism" that lives as if God is absent? What can you do right now to change this unhealthy perspective of God? Make a list of specific points of action.

4. "Where true faith is, the knowledge of God will be given as a fact of consciousness altogether apart from the conclusions of logic." What does Tozer mean by this statement? How has it been worked out in the lives of saints of the past and present? Try writing a new version of Tozer's statement, couching it in your own words.

5. Our God "does not distribute Himself that each may have a part, but to each one He gives all of Himself as fully as if there were no others. What a difference it makes when we cease being general (a dodge, incidentally, for pseudo-humility and unbelief) and become pointed and personal in our approach to God." How does the concept that God gives you "all of Himself as fully as if there were no others" affect the way you think about your relationship with

Him? If your faith in God seems too general and nonspecific, what could you do differently to make it more "pointed and personal"?

Chapter 5

Faith in the
Character of God

In our evangelical circles, faith is a theme upon which we like to dwell. No promise of God to answer prayer is more frequently quoted than the one we look at in this chapter. Jesus is speaking to His disciples:

> And whatsoever ye shall ask in my name, that will I do, that the Father may be glorified in the Son. If ye shall ask any thing in my name, I will do it. (John 14:13–14)

Some are concerned because there are not more miracles and wonders wrought in our midst through faith. In our day, everything is commercialized. And I must say that I do not believe in commercialized miracles.

"Miracles, Incorporated"—you can have it!

"Healing, Incorporated"—you can have that too! And the same with "Evangelism, Incorporated" and "Without a Vision the People Perish, Incorporated." I have my doubts about signs and wonders that have to be organized, that demand a letterhead and a president and a big trailer with lights and cameras. God is not in that!

But the person of faith who can go alone into the wilderness and get on his or her knees and command heaven—God is in that. The preacher who will dare to stand and let his preaching cost him something—God is in that. The Christian who is willing to put herself in a place where she must get the answer from God and God alone—the Lord is in that!

You must know by this time that I have a philosophy of faith. To begin with, I cannot recommend that anyone have faith in faith. We have a good amount of that notion abroad right now. There are preachers who devote themselves completely to preaching faith. As a result, people have faith in faith. They largely forget that our confidence must not be in the power of faith but in the Person and work of the Savior, Jesus Christ. So I have to confess that I cannot preach that way. I never have, and I never will. I know better.

In First John, the apostle writes out of divine inspiration: "And this is the confidence that we have in him, that, if we ask any thing according to his will, he heareth us: And if we know that he hear us, whatsoever we ask, we know that we have the petitions that we desired of him" (5:14–15).

God is the foundation of our faith

We have full confidence in Jesus Christ. He is the source and the foundation for all of our faith. In that kingdom of faith, we are dealing with Him, with God Almighty, the One whose essential nature is holiness, the One who cannot lie. Our confidence rises as the character of God becomes greater and more trustworthy to our spiritual comprehension. The One with whom we deal is the One who embodies faithfulness and truth.

So this is the confidence we have in Him. Faith mounts up on its heavenly wings, up toward the shining peaks, and says in satisfaction, "If God says it, I know it is so!" It is the character of God Himself, you see, that gives us this confidence.

I must again warn you of the great differences between today's evangelical rationalists and the evangelical mystics—the subject of our discussion in the previous chapter. I say there is a great difference between having confidence in God because of His character and trying to prove the things of God by human reason. We have evangelical rationalists today who insist on reducing everything to where it can be explained and proved. As a result, our faith is being rationized. And thus we pull almighty God down to the low level of human reason.

I am not insisting that human reason and faith in God are contrary to one another, but I do insist that one is above the other. When we are true believers in God's truth, we enter another world—a realm that is infinitely above reason.

> For my thoughts are not your thoughts, neither are your ways my ways, saith the LORD. For as the heavens are higher than the earth, so are my ways higher than your ways, and my thoughts than your thoughts. (Isaiah 55:8–9)

Faith never goes contrary to reason; faith simply ignores reason and rises above it.

Now, in dealing with these matters in the text, we must first go back to the plain statement of our Lord: "You may ask me for anything in my name, and I will do it." There is much praying being done among us that does not amount to anything. No possible good can come in our trying to cover up or deny it. The truth is that there is enough prayer made on any Sunday to save the whole world—but the world is not saved. About the only thing that comes back after our praying is the echo of our own voices. I contend that this kind of praying, so customary among us, has a most injurious effect upon the church of Christ.

Dangers in unanswered prayer

If unanswered prayer continues in a congregation over an extended period of time, the chill of discouragement will settle over the praying people. If we continue to ask and ask and ask, like petulant children, never expecting to get what we ask for but continuing to whine for it, we will become chilled within our beings.

If we continue in our prayers and never get answers, the lack of results will tend to confirm the natural unbelief of our hearts. Remember this: The human heart by nature is filled with unbelief. Unbelief, not disobedience, was the first sin. While disobedience was the first recorded sin, behind the act of disobedience was the sin of unbelief, else the act of disobedience would not have taken place.

The fact of unanswered prayer will also encourage the idea that religion is unreal, and this idea is held by many people in our day. "Religion is completely subjective," they tell us. "There is nothing real about it."

It is true that there may be nothing tangible to which religion can be referred. If I use the word *lake*, everyone thinks of a large body of water. When I use the word *star*, everyone thinks of a heavenly body. But when I use such words as *faith* and *belief* and *God* and *heaven*, there is not any image of a reality that is known to people and to which their minds immediately refer. To most people, those are just words—like *pixies* and *goblins*. So there is a false idea of unreality in our hearts when we pray and pray and pray and receive no answers.

Perhaps worst of all is the fact that our failures in prayer leave the enemy in possession of the field. The worst part about the failure of a military drive is not the loss of men or the loss of face but the fact that the enemy is left in possession of the field. In the spiritual sense, this is both a tragedy and a disaster. The devil ought to be on the run, always fighting a rearguard action. Instead, this blasphemous enemy smugly and scornfully holds his position, and the people of God let him have it. No wonder the work of the Lord is greatly retarded. Little wonder the work of God stands still!

Anything we ask for in His name

Dare we realize that Jesus said we can have anything we ask for in His name? John emphasizes that truth when he says, "This is the confidence—the boldness, the assurance—we have." I am not adding words, for the original Greek means all three: confidence, boldness, assurance. The word *confidence* is not sufficiently strong in English to convey the full meaning, so some translators have used the word *boldness* and others have used the word *assurance*.

It is right here that the person of faith and the person of reason come to the parting of the ways. This kind of teaching—that we can have confidence in God and He will give us what we ask in the name of Jesus—is flatly rejected by the person of unbelief. That person says it cannot be so, that it is unacceptable without the proof of human reason.

Unbelief is not just a mental attitude. It is a moral thing. Unbelief is always sinful because it always presupposes an immoral condition of the heart before it can exist. Unbelief is not the failure of the mind to grasp truth. It is not the unsoundness of a logical premise. It is not a bad conclusion drawn from a logical premise. It is a moral sin. People who say they cannot believe in the promises of God cannot understand this language with which we are dealing here. They say: "We must have a better reason for believing this than John's statement that God will hear us and answer us."

And yet, all of this time, as the argument goes on, the person of faith is confident. The person of faith does not dare rest on human reason. He or she does not reject the place of human reason, but he or she knows there are things that human reason cannot do.

Not against human reason

I have never been against human reason. I have only expressed myself against human reason's trying to do the things that human reason is not qualified to do. In every area where human reason is qualified, I say, "Turn human reason loose." You have a can opener in your house, and reason guides you in its use. In other words, you use the opener on cans, not to mend your little boy's socks. Nearly every home has a hammer and a saw in the garage or workroom. We know what they are for and how they should be used. We do not use them to paper the living room walls or to sweep the porch! If human reason is qualified, I say, use it. But there are some things human reason cannot do—things that are beyond its capacity.

Reason could not tell us that Jesus Christ should be born of a virgin, but faith knows that He was. Reason cannot prove that Jesus took upon Him the form of a man and that He died for the sins of the world, but faith knows that He did. Reason cannot prove that on the third day Jesus rose from the dead, but faith knows that it happened, for faith is an organ of knowledge. The rationalists take the position that the human brain alone is the organ of knowledge, but they either forget or overlook completely that feeling is a means of knowledge, and so is faith.

When the temperature outside is hot, we know it. Feeling is a means of knowledge. A young man loves a young woman. How does he know? Does he read the encyclopedia in order to base his love on reason? No, he listens to the ticking of his own heart. He knows it by feeling.

So, along with reason, feeling is a means of knowledge, and faith can be placed in the same category. This means that the person who has put his or her confidence in God has access to knowledge that the person who merely thinks and reasons cannot have.

Reason cannot say, "I know that Jesus will come to judge the living and the dead," but faith knows that He will do so. Reason cannot say, "My sins are gone," but faith knows that they are forgiven and forgotten. Faith simply ignores reason and rises above it. Intellect comes struggling along behind, like a little boy trying to keep up with his dad.

This is exactly why the word *wonder* often appears in the New Testament. "They wondered at him." "They wondered at him, and they all marvelled." Faith was going ahead, doing wonders, and reason was coming along, wide-eyed and amazed. This is the way it should be, always.

Short-legged reason

But in our day, we send reason ahead on its little short legs and faith never follows. Nobody marvels, because the whole business can be explained. I have always claimed that a believing Christian is a miracle, and at the precise moment that you can fully explain him, you have a Christian no longer! I have read the efforts of William James to psychologize the wonders of God's workings in the human life and experience. But the genuine child of God is someone who cannot be explained by human reasoning.

In this relationship with Jesus Christ through the new birth, something takes place by the ministry of the Spirit of God that psychology cannot explain. This is why I must contend that faith is the highest kind of reason after all, for faith goes straight into the presence of God. Our Lord Jesus Christ has gone ahead as a forerunner for us and engages God Almighty on our behalf. It is through this means alone that we may reach that for which we were created and finally commune with the Source of our being. We can love the Fountain of our life, praying to the One who has given us new birth. We can rest in the knowledge that God made heaven and earth.

We may not be astronomers, but we can know the God who made the stars. We may not be physicists, but we can know the God who made mathematics. There may be many technical and local bits of knowledge that we do not have, but we can know the God of all knowledge. We can enter beyond the veil into His very presence. There we stand hushed and wide-eyed as we gaze and gaze upon the wonders of Deity. It is faith that takes us there, and reason cannot disprove anything that faith discovers and knows. Reason can never do that.

Why should Christian writers think that they have to come to the help of almighty God? They are forever quoting a few scientific facts that, as they say, support the Bible. This is what good men are doing, but they are going in the wrong direction. Many of them are better men than I am, but they are wrong. Not all of the scientific facts ever assembled can support one spiritual fact; we are dealing with two different realms. One realm is reason and the other is faith in God.

If the sun should begin rising in the west and take its course to the east, if the summer should end abruptly and plunge us into the middle of winter without an autumn, if the corn in the fields started growing down instead of up—none of these things would change my mind about God or the Bible! I have not the words to emphasize strongly enough my position that faith in God is not dependent upon the support of any scientific helps.

Faith depends on God's character

No, we have confidence and boldness in God because He is God. We have learned enough about His character to know that we can lean upon Him fully.

You may have been told that if you will memorize more Bible verses, you will have more faith. I have been memorizing the Scriptures ever since I was converted, but my faith does not rest on God's promises. My faith rests upon God's character. Faith must rest in confidence upon the One who made the promises. It was written of Abraham that "he staggered not at the promise of God through unbelief; but was strong in faith, giving glory to God; and being fully persuaded that, what he had promised, he was able also to perform" (Romans 4:20–21). The glory went to God, not to the promise or to Abraham's faith.

So, what is the promise for? A promise is given to me so that I may know intelligently what God has planned for me, what God will give me, and so what to claim. Those are the promises, and they are intelligent directions. They rest upon the character and ability of the One who made them.

Let me illustrate. My estate consists principally of my books. I have a little household furniture but not too much and none of it too expensive. That and my books are about all I have. But suppose when my heirs gather to listen to the reading of my will, they hear, "I leave to my son Lowell a yacht in the Gulf of Mexico; I leave to my son Stanley an estate of one hundred acres in Florida; I leave to my son Wendell all the mineral rights that I hold in Nevada." You know what would happen, do you not? Those boys of mine, gathered for the reading of the will, would say in sympathy, "Poor Dad! He must have been mentally deranged to write a will like that! It is a meaningless will because he owned none of those things. He cannot make good on that will!"

But when the richest man in the country dies, and they call in the heirs, everyone listens closely for his or her own name because this is a will with resources behind it. The man has made the will in order that his heirs may know what they can claim. Just so, faith does not rest merely on promises. It goes back to the character of the one who makes the promises.

God cannot lie

Thus, when I read my Bible, I see this promise:

"If we ask any thing according to his will, he heareth us: And if we know that he hear us, whatsoever we ask, we know that we have the petitions that we desired of him" (1 John 5:14–15). That is a promise from God! I read the words of Jesus: "And whatsoever ye shall ask in my name, that will I do, that the Father may be glorified in the Son" (John 14:13). That is a promise from God!

Just how good are these promises? As good as the character of the One who made them. How good is that? Ah! This is our confidence. Faith says, "God is God!" He is a holy God who cannot lie, the God who is infinitely rich and can make good on all of His promises. He is the God who is infinitely honest. He has never cheated anyone! He is the God who is infinitely true. Just as good and true as God is—that is how good and true His promises are.

Where, then, do we make our mistake? What happens to our confidence?

We push the living God into a corner, trying to use Him as an escape from hell. We use Him to help us when the baby is sick—and then we go our own way. And after that we try to pump up faith by reading more promises in the Bible. But it will not work—I tell you that it will not work! We must be concerned with the person and character of God, not the promises. Through promises we learn what God has willed to us, we learn what we may claim as our heritage, we learn how we should pray. But faith itself must rest on the character of God.

Is this difficult to see? Why are we not stressing this in our evangelical circles? Why are we afraid to declare that people in our churches must come to know God Himself? Why do we not tell them that they must get beyond the point of making God a lifeboat for their rescue or a ladder to get them out of a burning building? How can we help our people get over the idea that God exists just to help run their businesses or fly their airplanes?

God is not a railway porter who carries your suitcase and serves you. God is God. He made heaven and earth. He holds the world in His hand. He measures the dust of the earth in the balance (see Isaiah 40:15). He spreads the sky out like a mantle. He is the great God Almighty. He is not your servant. He is your Father, and you are His child. He sits in heaven, and you are on the earth.

Why not more preaching about God?

When I think of the angels who veil their faces before the God who cannot lie, I wonder why every preacher in North America does not begin preaching about God—and nothing else. What would happen if every preacher just preached about the person and character of God for an entire year—who He is, His attributes, His perfection, His being, the kind of God He is and why we love Him and why we should trust Him? I tell you, God would soon fill the whole horizon, the entire world. Faith would spring up like grass by the water courses. Then let a man get up and preach the promises of God, and the whole congregation would join in chorus: "We can claim the promises; look who made them!" This is the confidence, this is the boldness.

Confidence may be slow in coming because we have been born and raised in an environment of lies. David "said in [his] haste, All men are liars" (Psalm 116:11). We do not read that he changed his mind after the stress had passed, because everyone has a deceitful heart, desperately wicked by nature (see Jeremiah 17:9). We are brought up in a world where lying is a fine art. Turn on the radio or television, and you will scarcely find an ad where the announcer can talk for twenty seconds without lying. We have become used to lies. The billboards lie. The magazines lie. This kind of deceit is all around us, and we pick it up without realizing it. We have lost our confidence in people.

If a man came to my door—a complete stranger—and said, "Pardon me, but because you are an upstanding citizen in this neighborhood, I am here to give you a hundred dollars," I would not take it. I would know there was a catch to it somewhere. We have come to expect the ruse in everything around us.

A young fellow stopped at the parsonage one day. "Good morning, Mr. Tozer!" That he knew my name did not surprise me; he could have learned it from the neighbor next door. He had a smile that you could not rub off. I inquired if he was selling magazines.

"Selling magazines?" he protested, acting as though I had wounded him deeply by my distrust. "I should say not!" But after about fifteen minutes of conversation, he admitted that it would help him through college if I could become interested in a magazine that he just happened to be able to furnish by subscription. But he was not selling magazines.

A psychology of deceit

For the most part, we live in a land of lies and deception. There is a psychology of deceit and mistrust ground into us from our birth. But when we enter the realm of the kingdom of God, the realm of faith, we find everything is different. Falsehoods and deceits are not known in heaven. Never in the blessed heavenly kingdom has anyone deceived another. The dear old Bible itself is a book of absolute honesty.

When Jesus was here upon the earth and walked among us, He used no fancy evangelistic maneuvers. He never said, "Now raise your hand; now put it down!" We have all heard about people who are supposed to be in Christian work, and we wonder if some of them are not scoundrels. Thank God, in His true kingdom there will be no dirty cheats who will take advantage of motherly old ladies. ("You remind me of my own praying mother. Will you pray with me? I need $500 to serve God." He knows she has the $500, and before he leaves she writes out the check, and he is on his way.)

I have more respect for the man who robs with a gun than for the cheating scoundrel who will take advantage of an unsuspecting person with his soft soap and hypocritical prayer. I feel it strongly. If there is any place in the whole world where people ought to be honest, it is in the church of God. I expect to so live and so preach that people can bring their friends to my church and assure them they can believe what they hear from my pulpit. I may be wrong sometimes, but I want always to be honest. As long as I have anything to say about it, any man who is a cheat will never have an invitation to put his feet down on the rug behind my pulpit!

Well, to repeat, the Bible always tells us the truth. God tells the whole story about men and women. He tells us what we would have covered up. The Bible tells us of David, a man after God's own heart, and it tells us how David fell, committing adultery. We would have left that chapter out, but God put it in. The Bible tells us about Peter, an apostle of the Lord. But Peter once swore that he never knew Jesus, and the Bible includes that detail.

Do not misuse the Bible

You can lean upon the Bible, its truth and its assurance in the things of God. You can trust it. But do not abuse it or misuse it. The Bible does not tell you that if you accept Christ you will have peace of mind. It does not tell you that because you are a Christian you are going to relax and sleep twelve hours a night. It does not tell you that you will suddenly become successful or that you will grow hair on your bald spot!

The Bible does tell you that you may have eternal life now—with hardship and crossbearing, but with glory in the world to come. The Bible makes it plain that if you are prepared to put up with the thorns and the crosses, the hardship and the hostility, you can have the crown.

That is what the Bible tells us. It is the good, honest old Book. No wonder God's saints die with the Bible at their side!

"I will do whatever you ask in my name. You may ask me for anything in my name." Asking in Jesus' name simply means asking according to His will. This is where the promises come in: You must know the promises to know what is His will. Memorize the Word of God; let it become a part of your being so that you can fully count upon the merit of Jesus.

The merit of Jesus is enough! We will enter paradise because Jesus went out from paradise on our behalf. We will live because Jesus died. We will be with God because Jesus was rejected from the presence of God in the terror of the crucifixion.

Our faith rests upon the character of God and the merit of His Son, Jesus. We do not have anything we can bring—only our poor, miserable souls. The bad person who thinks he or she is good is shut out of God's kingdom forever. But the person who knows he or she is the chief of sinners and totally unworthy, who comes in humility depending upon the merit of Jesus, enters in.

We cannot bargain with God

You cannot come to God with bargaining and with promises. But if you will throw yourself recklessly upon God, trust His character, trust the merits of His Son, you will have the petition you have asked of Him.

You can have this confidence in God, and you can have this respect for His will. Do not expect God to perform miracles for you so you can write books about them. Do not ever be caught asking God to send you toys like that to play around with.

But if you are in trouble and concerned about your situation and willing to be honest with God, you can have confidence in Him. You can go to Him in the merit of His Son, claiming His promises, and He will not let you down. God will help you, and you will find the way of deliverance.

God will move heaven and earth for you if you will trust Him.

Questions for Reflection
Faith in the Character of God

1. Our confidence in Christ "rises as the character of God becomes greater and more trustworthy to our spiritual comprehension." God Himself embodies all faithfulness and truth; our daily communion with Him is critical for faith to grow. Reflect on your times of communion with God during the past twenty-four hours. What aspects of God's character were most prominent to you during that time? How was your faith in Him affected?

2. "Faith never goes contrary to reason; faith simply ignores reason and rises above it." Meditate on this thought. Think of an example from your own life where you have seen this to be true.

3. Tozer notes that recurring seasons of unanswered prayer can breed doubt and unbelief in congregations and individual believers, until the things of God seem unreal or distant. However, God often allows such seasons of dryness to teach us patience, to test our faith or to refine our motives, among other things. Reflect on some of your own nonanswers to prayer and what God taught you about Himself.

4. If we have any understanding of the character of God, we will realize that we can trust Him fully. "My faith rests upon God's character. Faith must rest in confidence upon the One who made the promises." What promise of God have you been clinging to during the past weeks as you have prayed? What aspects of God's character are behind that promise? Evaluate whether your focus has been more on the promise instead of the God behind the promise.

5. "The heart is more deceitful than all else" (Jeremiah 17:9). One manifestation of such deceit is bargaining with God for answers to prayer. However, Tozer notes that we cannot bargain with God. Instead, if we throw ourselves recklessly upon God without escape routes, trust His character and trust the merits of His Son, we will have the petition we have asked of Him. Reflect on some situations where you had to trust Him completely for the results. What did you learn about God in those situations?

Chapter 6

God Is Easy to Live With

Satan's first attack upon the human race was his sly effort to destroy Eve's confidence in the kindness of God. Unfortunately for her and for us he succeeded too well. From that day, men have had a false conception of God, and it is exactly this that has cut out from under them the ground of righteousness and driven them to reckless and destructive living.

Nothing twists and deforms the soul more than a low or unworthy conception of God. Certain sects, such as the Pharisees, held that God was stern and austere, yet managed to maintain a fairly high level of external morality; but their righteousness was only outward. Inwardly they were "whited sepulchres," as our Lord Himself told them (Matthew 23:27). Their wrong conception of God resulted in a wrong idea of worship. To a Pharisee, the service of God was a bondage that he did not love but from which he could not escape without a loss too great to bear. The God of the Pharisee was not a God easy to live with, so his religion became grim and hard and loveless. It had to be so, for our notion of God must always determine the quality of our religion.

Much Christianity since the days of Christ's flesh has also been grim and severe. And the cause has been the same—an unworthy or an inadequate view of God. Instinctively we try to be like our God, and if He is conceived to be stern and exacting, so will we ourselves be.

From a failure properly to understand God comes a world of unhappiness among good Christians even today. The Christian life is thought to be a glum, unrelieved cross-carrying under the eye of a stern Father who expects much and excuses nothing. He is austere, peevish, highly temperamental and extremely hard to please. The kind of life that springs out of such libelous notions must of necessity be but a parody on the true life in Christ.

It is most important to our spiritual welfare that we hold in our minds always a right conception of God. If we think of Him as cold and exacting, we shall find it impossible to love Him, and our lives will be ridden with servile fear. If, again, we hold Him to be kind and understanding, our whole inner life will mirror that idea.

The truth is that God is the most winsome of all beings and His service one of unspeakable pleasure. He is all love, and those who trust Him need never know anything but that love. He is just indeed, and He will not condone sin; but through the blood of the everlasting covenant, He is able to act toward us exactly as if we had never sinned. Toward the trusting sons of men, His mercy will always triumph over justice.

The fellowship of God is delightful beyond all telling. He communes with His redeemed ones in an easy, uninhibited fellowship that is restful and healing to the soul. He is not sensitive or selfish nor temperamental. What He is today we shall find Him tomorrow and the next day and the next year. He is not hard to please, though He may be hard to satisfy. He expects of us only what He has Himself first supplied. He is quick to mark every simple effort to please Him, and just as quick to overlook imperfections when He knows we meant to do His will. He loves us for ourselves and values our love more than galaxies of new created worlds.

Unfortunately, many Christians cannot get free from their perverted notions of God, and these notions poison their hearts and destroy their inward freedom. These friends serve God grimly, as the elder brother did, doing what is right without enthusiasm and without joy, and seem altogether unable to understand the buoyant, spirited celebration when the prodigal comes home. Their idea of God rules out the possibility of His being happy in His people, and they attribute the singing and shouting to sheer fanaticism. Unhappy souls, these, doomed to go heavily on their melancholy way, grimly determined to do right if the heavens fall and to be on the winning side in the day of judgment.

How good it would be if we could learn that God is easy to live with. He remembers our frame and knows that we are dust (see Psalm 103:14). He may sometimes chasten us, it is true, but even this He does with a smile, the proud, tender smile of a Father who is bursting with pleasure over an imperfect but promising son who is coming every day to look more and more like the One whose child he is.

Some of us are religiously jumpy and self-conscious because we know that God sees our every thought and is acquainted with all our ways (see Psalm 139:2–3). We need not be. God is the sum of all patience and the essence of kindly goodwill. We please Him most, not by frantically trying to make ourselves good, but by throwing ourselves into His arms with all our imperfections, and believing that He understands everything and loves us still.

Questions for Reflection
God Is Easy to Live With

1. "Nothing twists and deforms the soul more than an unworthy conception of God." These defiled conceptions of God may come from our parents, our upbringing, our environment, our peers, our hard trials in life, our religious experiences, our arrogance or whatever. Tozer notes that such misconceptions undermine our worship of God and affect the quality of our religion. The right perspectives always come from the Word of God. Reflect on an unworthy conception of God that you have embraced at one time or another. What was the source of this misconception? What passages of Scripture helped you cast it off and put on the right perspective of God and His character?

2. One of the most common faulty conceptions of God is that of the servant with one talent in the parable of the talents (Matthew 25:14–30), who said, "Master, I knew you to be a hard man" (verse 24). Yet the Bible declares that our God is not hard, grim or severe, but is, in the words of Tozer, "the most winsome of all beings and His service one of unspeakable pleasure." Why do you think so many people, including believers, see God as hard and severe? How does this faulty image of God impede spiritual growth? Examine your own spiritual journey and determine if you need to root out any traces of this faulty image from your heart.

3.   Meditate on this description of God by Tozer: "He is not hard to please, though He may be hard to satisfy. He expects of us only what He has Himself first supplied. He is quick to mark every simple effort to please Him, and just as quick to overlook imperfections when He knows we meant to do His will. He loves us for ourselves and values our love more than galaxies of new created worlds." Is this the God that you have experienced in the past few weeks? If so, give Him the praise He deserves. If not, confess your unworthy concepts of God to Him and ask Him to restore in you a right perspective.

4.   Our concept of God will be mirrored in our inner life, and we often need others to tell us what we are reflecting. Spend some time with a very close spiritual friend or mentor and ask for help to see if you have reflected during the past months or years a clear and consistent image of Christ.

5.   "We please Him most, not by frantically trying to make ourselves good, but by throwing ourselves into His arms with all our imperfections, and believing that He understands everything and loves us still." Reflect on the freedom that this perspective of God brings to the Christian walk every day. Spend some time thanking and praising God that you are "accepted in the beloved" (Ephesians 1:6).

JOURNEY OF FAITH

Chapter 7

Faith Is a Journey, Not a Destination

They continued stedfastly in the apostles' doctrine and fellowship, and in breaking of bread, and in prayers. (Acts 2:42)

So says Luke of the thousands who received the Word and were baptized following the preaching of Peter on the day of Pentecost.

Conversion for those first Christians was not a destination; it was the beginning of a journey. And right there is where the biblical emphasis differs from ours.

Today all is made to depend upon the initial act of believing. At a given moment a "decision" is made for Christ, and after that everything is automatic. This is not taught in so many words, but such is the impression inadvertently created by our failure to lay a scriptural emphasis in our evangelistic preaching. We of the evangelical churches are almost all guilty of this lopsided view of the Christian life, and because the foundations are out of plumb, the temple of God leans dangerously and threatens to topple unless some immediate corrections are made.

In our eagerness to make converts, we allow our hearers to absorb the idea that they can deal with their entire responsibility once and for all by an act of believing. This is in some vague way supposed to honor grace and glorify God, whereas actually it is to make Christ the author of a grotesque, unworkable system that has no counterpart in the Scriptures of truth.

In the book of Acts, faith was for each believer a beginning, not an end; it was a journey, not a bed in which to lie while waiting for the day of our Lord's triumph. Believing was not a once-done act; it was more than an act—it was an attitude of heart and mind that inspired and enabled the believer to take up his cross and follow the Lamb whithersoever He went.

"They continued," says Luke, and is it not plain that it was only by continuing that they could confirm their faith? On a given day they believed, were baptized and joined themselves to the believing company. Very good, but tomorrow what? and the next day? and the next week? How could anyone know that their conversion had been genuine? How could they live down the critic's charge that they had been pressured into a decision? that they had cracked under the psychological squeeze set up by crowds and religious excitement? Obviously there was only one way: They continued.

Not only did they continue, they continued steadfastly. So wrote Luke, and the word *steadfastly* is there to tell us that they continued against serious opposition. Steadfastness is required only when we are under attack, mental or physical, and the story of those early Christians is a story of faith under fire. The opposition was real.

Here again is seen the glaring discrepancy between biblical Christianity and that of present-day evangelicals, particularly in the United States. In certain countries, I am told, some of our brethren are suffering painful persecution and counting not their lives dear unto themselves that they might win Christ. For these I have only utmost admiration. I speak not of such as they, but of the multitudes of religious weaklings within our evangelical fold here in America.

To make converts here, we are forced to play down the difficulties and play up the peace of mind and worldly success enjoyed by those who accept Christ. We must assure our hearers that Christianity is now a proper and respectable thing and that Christ has become quite popular with political bigwigs, well-to-do business tycoons and the Hollywood swimming pool set. Thus assured, hell-deserving sinners are coming in droves to "accept" Christ for what they can get out of Him; and though one now and again may drop a tear as proof of his sincerity, it is hard to escape the conclusion that most of them are stooping to patronize the Lord of glory much as a young couple might fawn on a boresome but rich old uncle in order to be mentioned in his will later on.

We will never be completely honest with our hearers until we tell them the blunt truth that as members of a race of moral rebels, they are in a serious jam and one they will not get out of easily. If they refuse to repent and believe in Christ, they will most surely perish; if they do turn to Him, the same enemies that crucified Him will try to crucify them. One way they suffer alone without hope; the other way they suffer with Christ for a while, but in the midst of their suffering they enjoy His loving consolation and inward support and are able to rejoice even in tribulation.

Those first believers turned to Christ with the full understanding that they were espousing an unpopular cause that could cost them everything. They knew they would henceforth be members of a hated minority group with life and liberty always in jeopardy.

This is no idle flourish. Shortly after Pentecost some were jailed, many lost all their earthly goods, a few were slain outright and hundreds "scattered abroad" (Acts 8:1).

They could have escaped all this by the simple expedient of denying their faith and turning back to the world; but this they steadfastly refused to do.

Seen thus in comparison with each other, is the Christianity of American evangelicalism today the same as that of the first century? I wonder. But again, I think I know.

Questions for Reflection
Faith Is a Journey, Not a Destination

1. "In the book of Acts, faith was for each believer a beginning, not an end; it was a journey, not a bed in which to lie while waiting for the day of our Lord's triumph." Take some time to reflect on your spiritual journey thus far; ask God to show you if you have been treating this challenging journey as more like "a bed in which to lie while waiting for the day of the Lord's triumph." Wait patiently by faith for the answer. If the Lord convicts you of a careless attitude toward your daily spiritual journey, acknowledge your sin, do not hide it or sugarcoat it, and allow Him to renew your faith.

2. Because walking by faith is a journey, continuing steadfastly in that daily journey confirms and strengthens our faith in Him. A believer trying to walk worthily will encounter opposition, setbacks, failure, discouragement, misunderstandings, false accusations and more. The true strength of our faith is measured by how we respond to these situations. How has your faith been affected by such things in the past six months—positively or negatively? What do you think could have put it more on the positive side?

3. Even if we realize that the walk of faith is a journey, it can be easy to fall into the sin of trying to coast—to seek our own comfort, to avoid conflict or battles, to enjoy our labors or blessings or to let others do what needs to be done. Why is this mind-set so dangerous in the journey of faith? In what ways have you been tempted to coast and not continue steadfastly to the end?

4. Have you suffered hardship or persecution for your faith? Have you lost a job or an opportunity for your stand in Christ? What impacts have these hardships had on your faith? Consider Tozer's description of the first-century church: "Those first believers turned to Christ with the full understanding that they were espousing an unpopular cause that could cost them everything. They knew they would henceforth be members of a hated minority group with life and liberty always in jeopardy." Such is happening more and more in the United States and is more common in many countries. Spend some time praying for those who are suffering for their faith, both here and abroad.

Chapter 8

Faith Is a Perturbing Thing

Faith," said the early Lutherans, "is a perturbing thing."

To Martin Luther goes the credit under God for having rediscovered the biblical doctrine of justification by faith. Luther's emphasis upon faith as the only way into peace of heart and deliverance from sin gave a new impulse of life to the decadent church and brought about the Reformation. That much is history. It is not a matter of opinion but of simple fact. Anyone can check it.

But something has happened to the doctrine of justification by faith as Luther taught it. What has happened is not so easily discovered. It is not a matter of simple fact, a plain yes or no, an obvious black or white. It is more elusive than that, and very much more difficult to come at; but what has happened is so serious and so vital that it has changed or is in the process of changing the whole evangelical outlook. If it comes, it may well turn Christianity inside out and put for the faith of our fathers something else entirely. And the whole spiritual revolution will be so gradual and so innocent-appearing that it will hardly be noticed. Anyone who fights it will be accused of jousting against windmills like Don Quixote.

The faith of Paul and Luther was a revolutionizing thing. It upset the whole life of the individual and made him into another person altogether. It laid hold on the life and brought it under obedience to Christ. It took up its cross and followed along after Jesus with no intention of going back. It said good-bye to its old friends as certainly as Elijah when he stepped into the fiery chariot and went away in the whirlwind. It had a finality about it. It snapped shut on a man's heart like a trap; it captured the man and made him from that moment forward a happy love-servant of his Lord. It turned earth into a desert and drew heaven within sight of the believing soul. It realigned all life's actions and brought them into accord with the will of God. It set its possessor on a pinnacle of truth from which spiritual vantage point he viewed everything that came into his field of experience. It made him little and God big and Christ unspeakably dear. All this and more happened to a man when he received the faith that justifies.

Came the revolution, quietly, certainly, and put another construction upon the word *faith*. Little by little the whole meaning of the word shifted from what it had been to what it is now. And so insidious was the change that hardly a voice has been raised to warn against it. But the tragic consequences are all around us.

Faith now means no more than passive moral acquiescence in the Word of God and the cross of Jesus. To exercise it we have only to rest on one knee and nod our heads in agreement with the instructions of a personal worker intent upon saving our soul. The general effect is much the same as that which men feel after a visit to a good and wise doctor. They come back from such a visit feeling extra good, withal smiling just a little sheepishly to think how many fears they had entertained about their health when actually there was nothing wrong with them. They just needed rest.

Such a faith as this does not perturb people. It comforts them. It does not put their hip out of joint so that they halt upon their thigh; rather it teaches them deep-breathing exercises and improves their posture. The face of their ego is washed and their self-confidence is rescued from discouragement. All this they gain, but they do not get a new name as Jacob did, nor do they limp into the eternal sunlight. "As he passed over Penuel the sun rose upon him" (Genesis 32:31). That was Jacob—rather, that was Israel, for the sun did not shine much upon Jacob. It was ashamed to. But it loved to rest upon the head of the man whom God had transformed.

This generation of Christians must hear again the doctrine of the perturbing quality of faith.

People must be told that the Christian religion is not something they can trifle with. The faith of Christ will command or it will have nothing to do with a man. It will not yield to experimentation. Its power cannot reach any man who is secretly keeping an escape route open in case things get too tough for him. The only man who can be sure he has true Bible faith is the one who has put himself in a position where he cannot go back. His faith has resulted in an everlasting and irrevocable committal, and however strongly he may be tempted, he always replies, "Lord, to whom shall we go? thou hast the words of eternal life" (John 6:68).

Questions for Reflection
Faith Is a Perturbing Thing

1. The walk of faith is not just a nice and comfortable journey of happiness. It is a life-changing journey where all actions and thoughts have been put into subjection to Christ, where the believer takes up the cross of Christ and is "little and God big and Christ unspeakably dear." Does this describe your walk of faith, or is this something that you have only heard of or read about from others? If your walk of faith has deviated from the biblical mandate, what can be done to get back on track?

2. Tozer declares that "faith now means no more than passive moral acquiescence in the Word of God and the cross of Jesus. . . . Such a faith as this does not perturb people. It comforts them." What are the dangers of this faulty perspective of faith for the individual believer and the church today? How does it affect our evangelism and our witness to the world around us?

3. "This generation of Christians," Tozer declares, "must hear again the doctrine of the perturbing quality of faith." Does your local church encourage your faith and stimulate you to trust God more? What opportunities do you have to meet with other believers who will challenge you in your faith?

What are some other methods or opportunities for growing your faith in Christ?

4. We tend to want to trust God only when we have no other choice. The spiritual reality is that all other avenues generally leave God out and are not God's best for us. Consider some situations in the past thirty days where you needed to trust God. Did you (if even unconsciously) have a fallback position if God didn't come through? Why is this perspective so undermining to true faith in God?

Chapter 9

True Faith Brings Commitment

To many Christians, Christ is little more than an idea, or at best an ideal; He is not a fact. Millions of professed believers talk as if He were real and act as if He were not. And always our actual position is to be discovered by the way we act, not by the way we talk.

We can prove our faith by our committal to it and in no other way. Any belief that does not command the one who holds it is not a real belief; it is a pseudobelief only. And it might shock some of us profoundly if we were brought suddenly face-to-face with our beliefs and forced to test them in the fires of practical living.

Many of us Christians have become extremely skillful in arranging our lives so as to admit the truth of Christianity without being embarrassed by its implications. We arrange things so that we can get on well enough without divine aid, while at the same time ostensibly seeking it. We boast in the Lord but watch carefully that we never get caught depending on Him. "The heart is deceitful above all things, and desperately wicked: who can know it?" (Jeremiah 17:9).

Pseudofaith always arranges a way out to serve in case God fails it. Real faith knows only one way and gladly allows itself to be stripped of any second way or makeshift substitutes. For true faith, it is either God or total collapse. And not since Adam first stood up on the earth has God failed a single man or woman who trusted Him.

The man of pseudofaith will fight for his verbal creed but refuse flatly to allow himself to get into a predicament where his future must depend upon that creed being true. He always provides himself with secondary ways of escape so he will have a way out if the roof caves in.

What we need very badly these days is a company of Christians who are prepared to trust God as completely now as they know they must do at the last day. For each of us the time is surely coming when we shall have nothing but God. Health and wealth and friends and hiding places will all be swept away, and we shall have only God. To the man of pseudofaith, that is a terrifying thought, but to real faith it is one of the most comforting thoughts the heart can entertain.

It would be a tragedy indeed to come to the place where we have no other but God and find that we had not really been trusting God during the days of our earthly sojourn. It would be better to invite God now to remove every false trust, to disengage our hearts from all secret hiding places and to bring us out into the open where we can discover for ourselves whether or not we actually trust Him. That is a harsh cure for our troubles, but it is a sure one. Gentler cures may be too weak to do the work. And time is running out on us.

Questions for Reflection
True Faith Brings Commitment

1. We seem to live in a culture that pays more attention to what one says than to what one does. In the church, Tozer says this is played out in our attitude toward Christ: "Millions of professed believers talk as if He were real and act as if He were not." Consider or give some examples of how a Christian might act as if Christ were not real. What effect does this have on a believer?

2. "Therefore as you have received Christ Jesus the Lord [by faith], so walk in Him" (Colossians 2:6) is the biblical mandate or model from our God. While we give mental assent to such a truth, Tozer says we arrange our lives to avoid being "embarrassed by its implications." What kinds of arrangements do believers make—at home, on the job, in our free time and our service to God—to avoid walking by faith? These temporary fleshly solutions never satisfy anyone permanently. What kind of changes in our day-to-day living would occur if we determined to trust God alone and consistently walk by faith?

3. Tozer comments that the man of pseudofaith always arranges a way out in case God fails. God never fails, but His timing, His ways and His process are often unexpected. God may test our faith through

apparent delays and setbacks, because He wants our faith to be pure and solid. Reflect back to a situation where it was difficult to wait for God's timing and solution. Were you tempted to look for a "way out"? What were the impacts on you and others around you as you waited on Him alone?

4. For sure, each of us has had or will have circumstances for which there is no solution but God. How are these situations a building block to faith in a great God?

Chapter 10

The Voice of Faith

*But now thus saith the L*ORD *that created thee, O Jacob, and he that formed thee, O Israel, Fear not: for I have redeemed thee, I have called thee by thy name; thou art mine. When thou passest through the waters, I will be with thee; and through the rivers, they shall not over-flow thee: when thou walkest through the fire, thou shalt not be burned; neither shall the flame kindle upon thee. For I am the L*ORD *thy God, the Holy One of Is-rael, thy Saviour: I gave Egypt for thy ransom, Ethiopia and Seba for thee. (Isaiah 43:1–3)*

What God has ever done for anyone He will do for anybody else. Let us get a hold of this and not write the lives of our fathers and gild the sepul-chres of the ones who have gone before, imagining that we live in a vacuum, void of those who have experienced God. Anything God ever did for anyone in faith He will do for anyone else who meets His conditions.

The voice of unbelief says, "Yes, I'm a believer. I believe the Bible. I don't like those modernists, liberals and modern scientists who deny the Bible. I would not do that for the world. I believe in God, and I believe that God will bless." That is, He will bless at some other time, in some other place and some other people. Those are three sleepers that bring the work of God to a halt. We are believers, and we can quote the creed with approval. We believe it, but we believe that God will bless some other people, some other place, some other time— but not now, not here and not us.

Here is the problem: We have to have faith if God is going to do anything for us. Faith is the vitamin that makes all we take from the Bible digestible and makes us able to receive it and assimilate it. If we do not have faith, we cannot get anything. If we allow the gloomy voice of unbelief to whisper to us that God will bless some other time but not now, some other place but not here, some other people but not us, we might as well turn off the lights because nobody will get anywhere.

The voice of faith, however, has quite another message for us. The voice of faith speaks up brightly, though reverently, and says, "Anything God promised and did at any time in any place for anybody God will do for us here if we will meet His conditions." This is basic. When God speaks, His message has more than one application. If it is truth, it is true for anybody who would believe it anywhere, anytime. Two times two equals four whether it is 400 BC or AD 1963, whether in Russia, in China or in Canada. Two times two equals four. No one can get around it; anybody can trust it. Nobody can dispensationalize it away. It is an unchanging principle.

When God speaks and His mighty voice thunders down the years, He speaks to His people called Israel and He speaks to His people called Christians. Nothing has happened to invalidate His promises. We must remember that. Nothing in history would invalidate the promises of God. Nothing in philosophy, nothing that science has ever discovered can invalidate His promises. Certainly there have been social changes, and people look at things differently now than they did in other times. Nevertheless, nothing changes God, His promises, human nature, God's purposes or His intentions toward His people, so we can take the Word of God and say, "Here is a living Word."

The first sentence of the Scripture passage says, "Thus saith the LORD." Many Bible translations print the word *Lord* in capital letters. This indicates that the Hebrew word used is *Jehovah* or *Yahweh*.

The name *Yahweh* is sometimes called the tetragrammaton. It is so sacred that ancient Jews would not even speak it. It was the name God spoke out of the fire to Moses when He said, "I AM THAT I AM" (Exodus 3:14). That is who is speaking in this passage. Can He make good on His intentions? He certainly can.

Seven names with Jehovah

In our hymnody, books of devotion and important books of theology there are seven names that God gives in compound with Jehovah.

First, *Jehovah-jireh* means "the Lord will provide." If the people of God would remember this, "I am that I am" will provide. He who laid the foundation of the earth, who stretched the heavens above like a curtain and who looks upon the nations and sees them as dust in the balance will provide.

Second, *Jehovah-rapha* means "the Lord who heals you." This is the expression that A.B. Simpson picked up and gave meaning to so it could shine through again. "I am the Lord who heals you." We do not see much or hear much about that now. The doctrine of divine healing is divided into two classes: those who are making a circus out of it, and the discouraged people who are trying to believe and take pills to beat sickness. There is very little of real knowledge of *Jehovah-rapha*, the God who heals, anymore.

Then there is *Jehovah-nissi*, "the Lord our banner"; *Jehovah-shalom*, "The Lord our peace"; *Jehovah-ro'i*, "the Lord our shepherd"; *Jehovah-tsidkenu*, "the

Lord our righteousness"; and *Jehovah-shammah*, "the Lord is present here." This is the mighty God who is speaking, and He wants to get through to you.

Fed trash too many times

Do you know you have been fed trash instead of truth too many times? Do you know you have been betrayed and sold downriver instead of being fed the living Word of God in too many instances? God is trying to get through to you in His Word, and He says, "I am Jehovah. You are looking to me now. Look away from other people; look to me."

Who are the people we look to? They may be young and good-looking today, but tomorrow they will be old and crack-voiced. But the great God Almighty does not die. "I am Jehovah; I am your righteousness; I am your shepherd; I am your peace; I am your banner of victory; I am your healer; I am your provider; I am present in your midst." This is the One with whom you are dealing. If you would only dare to rise, shake your head and say, "I dare to believe this," you would find the truths of God begin to glow like the stars. You would have life where you have not life, light where you have not light and joy where you have not joy.

What did God do?

I, even I, am the LORD; and beside me there is no saviour. I have declared, and have saved, and I have shewed, when there was no strange god among you: therefore ye are my witnesses, saith the LORD, that I am God. Yea, before the day was I am he; and there is none that can deliver out of my hand: I will work, and who shall let it?

Thus saith the LORD, your redeemer, the Holy One of Israel; For your sake I have sent to Babylon, and have brought down all their nobles, and the Chaldeans, whose cry is in the ships. I am the LORD, your Holy One, the creator of Israel, your King. Thus saith the LORD, which maketh a way in the sea, and a path in the mighty waters; which bringeth forth the chariot and horse, the army and the power; they shall lie down together, they shall not rise: they are extinct, they are quenched as tow. (Isaiah 43:11–17)

The great God Almighty is the God of history. And what will He do now?

Behold, I will do a new thing; now it shall spring forth; shall ye not know it? I will even make a way in the wilderness, and rivers in the desert. The beast of the field shall honour me, the dragons and the owls: because I give waters in the wilderness, and rivers in the desert, to give drink to my people, my chosen. (43:19–20)

I believe that God has some chosen ones, and that God wants to bring drink to His chosen ones. To bring this to our church, we need to do a few things. One is to repudiate unbelief. The average evangelical church lies under a shadow of quiet doubting. The doubt is not the unbelief that argues against Scripture, but worse than that. It is chronic unbelief that does not know what faith means.

There is a difference between the unbeliever who does not believe the Bible, boldly says so and argues against it and the so-called Christian who simply lies in a state of coma and cannot rise and believe. It is like the difference between a man who has had an accident or becomes suddenly ill and the chronic invalid who never knows what it is to be quite well, but who is not quite dead. The invalid can always muster a smile and does have a heartbeat, but the person is not normal. He does have a temperature and respiration, but he is not normal. The person is not alive, but, thank God, he is not dead, either.

The person who hits the abutment of the road doing sixty miles per hour is still warm although dead. Drag such a person out and he or she is still warm—but dead. Death happened suddenly and dramatically. Likewise, something dramatic and terrible has happened to the person who says, "I don't believe your Bible. It's a saga of old notions. It's filled with stories of adultery and murder and assassination. I don't believe your Bible." He or she has hit something hard and has been injured.

A state of chronic unbelief

But the churches lie around in a state of chronic unbelief. They do not expect God to do anything, and naturally He does not. On occasion one will be added to the church by mulling and wooing and needling and pawing over the person until we get him or her in. But the lift, freedom, brightness and joy of the true Christian who believes God is missing from us.

The voice of unbelief comes out of the psychology of nonexpectation. This is our trouble these days: the psychology of nonexpectation. So we sit down to have a board meeting. What are we going to do to stir ourselves up? Who can we get?

Where will we look? We forget that all the time Jehovah is present. "I am Jehovah-shammah. I am in the midst of you. Why don't you talk to me?" No, we don't ask Him.

"I am your banner of victory." But we say, "I just wonder how much it will cost?" How much does a revival cost? Absolutely nothing and absolutely everything—that is how much it will cost. It will cost not one dime, and it will cost everything we have. You cannot import it by flying someone in from New Zealand. How many of these blessed preachers have come in from Ireland and England? They did some big things over there, we heard, so we flew them in and they never got anywhere. I never saw anything result from trying to import God. He does not fly over in a jet. He says, "I am Jehovah; I am with you. I am where you are; I am here now. Call on Me."

"But thou hast not called upon me," He says

next. "But thou hast not called upon me, O Jacob; but thou hast been weary of me, O Israel" (Isaiah 43:22). In other words, we are bored with God Almighty. We chuckle at Pogo and laugh at Dear Abby, but we are bored with God. "You are weary of Me; you are bored with Me." I do not hesitate to say that much of what is going on in the name of Christianity today is simply boredom.

God says, "Why don't you call on Me? I am here, and I am ready to help you. I will do these things for you." The voice of unbelief says, "Things will be as they are. There is no use." But the voice of Jehovah says, "Behold, I will do a new thing. . . . I will even make a way in the wilderness, and rivers in the desert" (Isaiah 43:19).

Unbelief is entirely logical and true to nature. People of faith, however, have a logic that is higher than natural logic, a logic that cannot be seen by unbelievers. But unbelief is entirely logical. The sun rises, and the sun also sets. It rains and it snows. Seasons follow each other. The ducks fly to the north and then to the south. Babies are born and old men die. Things go on as they go on. "As it was in the beginning, is now and ever shall be"—that is the only hymn we know. Things will be as they have been, we sing in unbelief.

"Behold, I will"

But the voice of Jehovah says, "Behold, I will." When you introduce God, a new thing happens.

"I will even make a way in the wilderness." Who ever heard of it? "And rivers in the desert." Who ever heard of it? Unbelief is logical and true to nature because nature is fixed in a regular routine. You may expect nature to continue to go right on in that routine. However, another factor is now introduced. God introduces the supernatural, and He says, "I am who I am and I will." God wills to do a new thing.

We keep going the way of nature in the fixed routine. You cannot expect anybody to do anything about it. But I hear another voice saying, "I am that I am." Since I have been a Christian, I have lived for that voice. I have lived to hear God say, "I am that am. You can't, but I can. You aren't, but I am. You are not able, but I am able. You have no wisdom, but I am Jehovah and I have the wisdom."

We approach Him through Jesus Christ His Son. Never forget that all the power of this great Jehovah with His awful and awesome glorious names is channeled through the person of His Son, Jesus Christ, to His people. Jesus dug a channel, so to speak, through to the mighty ocean that is Jehovah so all the sweet waters, the healing waters, the soul-quenching waters that are God can flow down to the Lord's people if they would only believe.

God does not say that this is new to Him. Nothing is new to God; it is just new to us. When God says to us, "I will do a new thing," what is it? Is God going to create something brand new as though He were creating a galaxy out of nothing? No, He is going to repeat for a new generation what He did for an old generation. He says, "I will do it for you. Why do you worry? I will do it for you. I am God. I am Jehovah. I am your righteousness. I am your provider. I am your healer. I am your banner of victory. I am your shepherd. I am your peace. I am your everything."

If God is all this to us, then there is no reason why anybody should be downhearted in this hour. If God could make a world out of nothing, why can't He make anything He wants now for His people? God invites us to see Him work.

God will do it in such a way that nobody gets the glory but Himself. God is going to get the glory, and He is not going to share it with anybody. "I am the LORD . . . , and my glory will I not give to another"(Isaiah 42:8). (See also Isaiah 49:11.) God wants to do things in a way that nobody can say somebody else did it. God is doing it because He wants the glory and must have the glory because of who He is. He says, "I will make." We need a God who can make things; we need a God who can create, and He invites us to watch Him create.

Don't allow your past to paralyze you

Do not let any of the things of the world or past mistakes paralyze your hearts. I believe there are Christians who have allowed some of their past mistakes to paralyze them. You were so bright and cheerful in your spiritual life once, and then you made some tragic mistake or had something happen to you. You got out of it somehow, and prayed and wept your way out of it. But it did something to you, and now you cannot lick it. Past wrongs that have been done to you, past failures, times you thought you were going to win and did not, or present sins or discouragement—these things are not mental at all. They are deeper than that; they are subconscious, and they prevent us from believing.

I most urgently exhort you, and I trust God Almighty to deliver you; to sponge that out of your spirit; to sponge that out of your heart so you are not hindered by unbelief. The simple people of the world can believe God in a way that we who are more sophisticated have a hard time doing. That is why God has to begin with the simple people. Jesus could not get the Pharisees to follow Him, but He did get some fishermen and some simple people. He got one tax collector, but He did not get very many great people. God comes to simple people.

If we could shake off our sophistication, our pseudo learning and the cheap crust of unbelief that is over us, we could hear Him say, "I am that I am, and I am with you. I am on your side. My Son died for you, and hell cannot take you out of My hands. You are made for My glory. I formed you for Myself to praise Me. If you will only believe, I will give you waters in the wilderness and rivers in the desert. I will give drink to My people, My chosen. I will do these things for you."

An element of the supernatural enters here. Nature says it cannot be, and nature is right. But God steps in and says, "I am that I am, and it can be." And God is right. I cannot win against my enemies, but God says, "I will be an enemy unto thine enemies, and an adversary unto thine adversaries" (Exodus 23:22).

If we will unite our hearts and intentions and dare to believe it, we will see God begin to move in great strength and in great power. We will see coming down from heaven that which we so desperately struggled to bring in from the outside. We will see the great God do it and then it will not be said, "This man did it," or "That woman did it." But we can all say together, "Not by might, nor by power, but by my spirit, saith the LORD of hosts" (Zechariah 4:6).

Questions for Reflection
The Voice of Faith

1. The voice of unbelief manifests itself when the true Christian listens to the whispers that God "will bless at some other time, in some other place and some other people." Tozer notes that these three sleepers bring the work of God to a halt in our lives. We must have faith in God if God is going to do anything for us. Think back to a recent situation where the voice of unbelief impacted your waiting, your actions, or your progress in Christ. What should have been done differently? Confess and repent of any action that was not of faith and move on in the power of the Holy Spirit.

2. The names of God are microcosms of the character and person of God. Why should we memorize and meditate on these names of God? How does such reflection on God affect our hearing His voice daily and walking by faith? Read Isaiah 50:10 for another reason for reflection on the names of God.

3. Tozer notes that "the churches lie around in a state of chronic unbelief" and that "chronic unbelief does not know what faith is." But if we, as individuals or corporately as a church, listen to the voice of unbelief, we do not expect God to do anything, and we seek our own solutions instead of trusting Him. The

impact of such unbelief undermines our awe of God, affects our current relationship with Him, damages our testimony before others and destroys our walk of faith. Think of a time when you failed to believe God. What were the consequences of that unbelief? How did God restore you?

4. "Anything God promised and did at any time in any place for anybody God will do for us here if we will meet His conditions." What are the conditions that Tozer is talking about? Take some time to read and meditate on the following passages: James 1:5–7; Psalm 27:14; Psalm 66:18; James 4:3. What actions can you take to be faithful to the conditions this week?

5. It is critical to not allow our past to paralyze us in the walk of faith: past sins, past mistakes, past victories, past failures, past wrongs done to us and more. God is greater than all of our past, bad and good; and He can use it all for our good if we would but trust Him only. Thank God for your past, your present circumstances and for your future. Make a vow right now and ask God to enable you to keep the vow to put aside all that is behind and to press forward for His glory.

Chapter 11

We Must Hear Worthily

It is carelessly assumed by most persons that when a preacher pronounces a message of truth and his words fall upon the ears of his listeners, there has been a bona fide act of hearing on their part. They are assumed to have been instructed because they have listened to the Word of God. But it does not follow.

If we would be truly instructed, we must be worthy to hear; or more accurately, we must hear in a worthy manner. In listening to a sermon, reading a good book or even reading the Bible itself, much may be lost to us because we are not worthy to hear the truth—that is, we have not met the moral terms required to hear the truth rightly.

The text, "So shall my word be that goeth forth

out of my mouth: it shall not return unto me void"
(Isaiah 55:11), does not give support to the notion
that God's truth is effective wherever and whenever it is preached. The lament of the Old Testament prophets was that they cried aloud unto Israel and their words were not regarded. "Because
I have called, and ye refused; I have stretched out
my hand, and no man regarded; but ye have set
at nought all my counsel, and would none of my
reproof" (Proverbs 1:24–25). Our Lord's parable of
the sower and the seed is another proof that it is
possible to hear truth without profit. Paul turned
from the Jews with the quotation, "Hearing ye shall
hear, and shall not understand" (Acts 28:26), and
began his ministry to the Gentiles.

Before there can be true inward understanding
of divine truth, there must be a moral preparation.
Our Lord made this plain in several passages in the
Gospels. "At that time Jesus answered and said,
I thank thee, O Father, Lord of heaven and earth,
because thou hast hid these things from the wise
and prudent, and hast revealed them unto babes.
Even so, Father: for so it seemed good in thy sight"
(Matthew 11:25–26). The Gospel according to John
is filled with the teaching that there must be a spiritual readying within the soul before there can be a
real understanding of God's truth. This is summed
up in 7:17, "If any man will do his will, he shall
know of the doctrine." And Paul said plainly, "But
the natural man receiveth not the things of the Spir-

it of God: for they are foolishness unto him: neither can he know them, because they are spiritually discerned" (1 Corinthians 2:14).

When considering a pastor, the average church asks, in effect, "Is this man worthy to speak to us?" I suppose such a question is valid, but there is another one more in keeping with the circumstances; it is, "Are we worthy to hear this man?" An attitude of humility on the part of the hearers would secure for them a great deal more light from whatever sized candle the Lord might be pleased to send them.

When a man or woman becomes worthy to hear, God sometimes talks to them through very unworthy media. Peter, as an example, was brought to repentance by the crowing of a rooster. Of course the rooster was innocent of the part he was playing, but Peter's Lord had set things up for him so that the rooster's crow could break the heart of His backslidden apostle and send him out in a flood of penitential tears. Augustine was brought to repentance by seeing a friend killed by lightning. Nicholas Hermann was converted through seeing a tree stripped of its leaves in winter. Spurgeon became a Christian after hearing a humble Methodist class leader exhort a congregation. Moody was led into a clear anointing of the Spirit through the testimony of a simple-hearted elderly lady of his acquaintance.

All these examples teach the same thing. God

will speak to the hearts of those who prepare themselves to hear; and conversely, those who do not so prepare themselves will hear nothing even though the Word of God is falling upon their outer ears every Sunday.

Good hearers are as important as good preachers. We need more of both.

Questions for Reflection
We Must Hear Worthily

1. Have you ever wondered why you have heard certain biblical truths time after time and nothing ever clicked in your heart of hearts? Why is it after so much repetition of a specific truth that we finally cling to it and experience a peace and rest in Christ that is beyond description? If you have had this situation happen to you lately, reflect on what God is trying to accomplish in your walk of faith.

2. To hear worthily, Tozer notes that "before there can be true inward understanding of divine truth, there must be a moral preparation." What are the aspects of this daily preparation that must be ingrained in our lives by the Spirit in order to hear worthily?

3. "God will speak to the hearts of those who prepare themselves to hear; and conversely, those who do not so prepare themselves will hear nothing even though the Word of God is falling upon their outer ears every Sunday." Basically, one cannot really hear the Lord once a week unless they have prepared themselves to hear Him every day in many ways. List the different ways you heard from the Lord this week.

4. "For everyone who partakes only of milk is not accustomed to the word of righteousness, for he is an infant. But solid food is for the mature, who because of practice have their senses trained to discern good and evil" (Hebrews 5:13–14). The one who is truly walking by faith will not stay a babe long, will hunger for divine truth, will discern good and evil, will avoid soft or watered-down truth and will gravitate to books and people who have known and experienced the Lord and His ways deeply. In light of this last statement, assess your walk of faith. Are you growing? Are you hungering for truth? Are you discerning, avoiding the wrong and gravitating toward the good?

Chapter 12

Laboring the Obvious

Many of us who preach the unsearchable riches of Christ are often pretty dull and hard to listen to.

The freshest thought to visit the human mind should be the thought of God. The story of salvation should put a radiancy in the face and a vibrancy in the voice of him who tells it. Yet it is not uncommon to hear the wondrous message given in a manner that makes it difficult for the hearer to concentrate on what is being said. What is wrong?

The conventional answer, "The speaker is not full of the Holy Spirit," does not tell us enough. Many who by every test of life and love are temples of the Spirit manage to sound like a worn-out phonograph record that was not very good in the first place.

It is true that only the Spirit-filled preacher can be morally effective at last; but for the moment we are thinking only of the ability of a speaker to command the attention of his hearers. And if the speaker cannot keep his hearers immediately interested, his message cannot possibly have a long-range effect upon them, no matter how spiritual he may be.

Probably no other part of the Holy Scriptures has suffered as much from dull exposition as have the epistles of Paul. The writings themselves are gems of beauty, lyrical and musical. Sermons based on them should be "as crisp as biting into a fresh apple." Instead they are often as disappointing as biting into a ball of yarn. Why?

It would probably be an oversimplification to name any single cause as being alone responsible for the dullness of our preaching, but I nevertheless venture to suggest that one very important factor is our habit of laboring the obvious. (If any reader should smile and say, "That is what this editorial is doing," I have no defense to offer. At least I see my fault and shall try to remedy it.)

In trying to discover the cause of my aversion to the ministry of certain evangelical Bible teachers, I have concluded that it is their incurable habit of laboring the obvious. They seem not to know that elementary truths often repeated dull the spiritual faculties of the saints. Especially is this true when the teacher insists upon playing with theological blocks, spelling out the first principles of the doctrine of Christ apparently with no intention of going on.

The vast majority of our Bible conferences are dedicated to the obvious. Each of the brethren (usually advertised as "widely sought after as a conference speaker") ranges afar throughout the Scriptures to discover additional passages to support truth already known to and believed by 99 percent of his hearers. If the speaker can show that some elementary truth had been hidden in an Old Testament "type" and not before noticed, he is hailed as a profound Bible scholar and eagerly invited back next year.

This engrossment in first principles has an adverse effect upon the evangelical church. It is as if an intelligent child should be forced to stay in the third grade five or six years. The monotony is just too great. The mind cannot remain alert when the elements of surprise and disclosure are missing. Personally I sit through the average orthodox sermon with the same sense of bored frustration one might feel who was reading a mystery story through for the twelfth time.

Our tendency to repeat endlessly a half dozen basic doctrines is the result of our lack of prophetic insight and our failure to meet God in living encounter. The knowledge of God presents a million facets, each one shining with a new ravishing light. The teacher who lives in the heart of God, reads Scriptures with warm devotion, undergoes the discipline and chastisement of the Holy Spirit and presses on toward perfection is sure every now and again to come upon fresh and blessed vistas of truth, old indeed as the Word itself, but bright as the dew on the grass in the morning. The heart that has seen the far glimpses of advanced truth will never be able to keep quiet about them. His experiences will get into his sermons one way or another, and his messages will carry an element of surprise and delight altogether absent from the ordinary Bible talks heard everywhere these days.

Something within the heart of the normal man revolts against motion without progress. Yet this is precisely what we are offered in the vast majority of evangelical churches. Doctrinally these churches are moving around a tight and narrow circle. Their teachers tell them that this circle encompasses all the land of Beulah and warn them of the danger of looking for anything more.

The teaching that consists entirely of reiteration cannot but be dull and wearisome; so the churches try to make up for the religious lassitude they cannot help but feel by introducing extrascriptural diversions and antiscriptural entertainments to provide the stultified saints with a bit of relish for their tedium. It never seems to occur to anyone that there is true joy farther on if they would only escape from the circle and strike out for the hills of God.

To bring news already known; to marshal texts

to prove truth everyone believes and no one disputes; to illustrate by endless stories doctrines long familiar; to lay again and again the foundations of repentance from dead works and faith toward God—this is to labor the obvious.

"Therefore leaving the principles of the doctrine of Christ, let us go on unto perfection" (Hebrews 6:1).

Questions for Reflection
Laboring the Obvious

1. Tozer notes that many evangelical Bible teachers
    "seem not to know that elementary truths often
    repeated dull the spiritual faculties of the saints."
    Hebrews 5:11–12 says "Concerning him [Christ] we
    have much to say, and it is hard to explain, since
    you have become dull of hearing. For though by this
    time you ought to be teachers, you have need again
    for someone to teach you the elementary principles
    of the oracles of God, and you have come to need
    milk and not solid food." Consider for a moment
    if much of the biblical teaching you have been ex-
    posed to has been a laboring of the obvious. What
    has been the impact on you, your attitude and your
    walk of faith? What actions can you take to remedy
    the situation?

2. Tozer notes that Bible teachers who have a "tenden-
    cy to repeat endlessly a half dozen basic doctrines"
    show a "lack of prophetic insight" and a "failure
    to meet God in living encounter." What should a
    Christian do to avoid such teachers? How should a
    church member pray for leaders who have this ten-
    dency?

3. Tozer notes that "the heart that has seen the far
    glimpses of advanced truth will never be able to

keep quiet about them." What advanced truth have you heard from God's lips lately that you cannot keep quiet about? The ingraining of that truth into the life is critical to being prepared to hear the next truth. If you have not received an advanced truth lately, spend some time in prayer, asking the Holy Spirit to lead you into all truth.

4. "The teaching that consists entirely of reiteration cannot but be dull and wearisome; so the churches try to make up for the religious lassitude they cannot help but feel by introducing extrascriptural diversions and antiscriptural entertainments to provide the stultified saints with a bit of relish for their tedium." What kinds of reiterated teaching, diversions and entertainments is Tozer referring to? How should we judge the value of a particular church activity or event?

ACTION OF FAITH

Chapter 13

Religion Should Produce Action

The supreme purpose of the Christian religion is to make men like God in order that they may act like God. In Christ the verbs *to be* and *to do* follow each other in that order.

True religion leads to moral action. The only true Christian is the practicing Christian. Such a one is in very reality an incarnation of Christ as Christ is the incarnation of God; not in the same degree and fullness of perfection, for there is nothing in the moral universe equal to that awful mystery of godliness that joined God and man in eternal union in the person of the Man Christ Jesus; but as the fullness of the Godhead was and is in Christ, so Christ is in the nature of the one who believes in Him in the manner prescribed in the Scriptures.

God always acts like Himself wherever He may be and whatever He may be doing. When God became flesh and dwelt among us, He did not cease to act as He had been acting from eternity. "He veiled His deity but He did not void it." The ancient name dimmed down to spare the helpless eyes of mortal men, but as much as was seen was true fire. Christ restrained His powers, but He did not violate His holiness. In whatsoever He did, He was holy, harmless, separate from sinners and higher than the highest heaven.

Just as in eternity God acted like Himself and when incarnated in human flesh still continued in all His conduct to be true to His holiness, so does He when He enters the nature of a believing man. This is the method by which He makes the redeemed man holy. He enters a human nature at regeneration as He once entered human nature at the incarnation and acts as becomes God, using that nature as a medium of expression for His moral perfections.

Cicero, the Roman orator, once warned his hearers that they were in danger of making philosophy a substitute for action instead of allowing it to produce action. What is true of philosophy is true also of religion. The faith of Christ was never intended to be an end in itself nor to serve instead of something else. In the minds of some teachers, faith stands in lieu of moral conduct and every inquirer after God must take his choice between the two. We are presented with the well-known either/

or: Either we have faith or we have works, and faith saves while works damn us. Hence the tremendous emphasis on faith and the apologetic, mincing approach to the doctrine of personal holiness in modern evangelism. This error has lowered the moral standards of the church and helped to lead us into the wilderness where we currently find ourselves.

Rightly understood, faith is not a substitute for moral conduct but a means toward it. The tree does not serve in lieu of fruit but as an agent by which fruit is secured. Fruit, not trees, is the end God has in mind in yonder orchard; so Christlike conduct is the end of Christian faith. To oppose faith to works is to make the fruit the enemy to the tree; yet that is exactly what we have managed to do. And the consequences have been disastrous.

A miscalculation in laying the foundation of a building will throw the whole superstructure out of plumb, and the error that gave us faith as a substitute for action instead of faith in action has raised up in our day unsymmetrical and ugly temples of which we may well be ashamed and for which we shall surely give a strict account in the day when Christ judges the secrets of our hearts.

In practice we may detect the subtle (and often unconscious) substitution when we hear a Christian assure someone that he will "pray over" his problem, knowing full well that he intends to use prayer as a substitute for service. It is much easier to pray that a poor friend's needs may be supplied than to supply them. James' words burn with irony: "If a brother or sister be naked, and destitute of daily food, and one of you say unto them, Depart in peace, be ye warmed and filled; notwithstanding ye give them not those things which are needful to the body; what doth it profit?" (James 2:15–16). And the mystical John sees also the incongruity involved in substituting religion for action: "But whoso hath this world's good, and seeth his brother have need, and shutteth up his bowels of compassion from him, how dwelleth the love of God in him? My little children, let us not love in word, neither in tongue; but in deed and in truth. And hereby we know that we are of the truth, and shall assure our hearts before him" (1 John 3:17–19).

A proper understanding of this whole thing will destroy the false and artificial either/or. Then we will have not less faith but more godly works; not less praying but more serving; not fewer words but more holy deeds; not weaker profession but more courageous possession; not a religion as a substitute for action but religion in faith-filled action.

And what is that but to say that we will have come again to the teaching of the New Testament?

Questions for Reflection
Religion Should Produce Action

1. "The supreme purpose of the Christian religion is
    to make men like God in order that they may act
    like God. In Christ the verbs *to be* and *to do* follow
    each other in that order." In Christ, the two extremes
    of "being" or "doing" undermine the walk of faith.
    Which extreme do you gravitate to? What are the
    consequences of continually leaning toward the ex-
    tremes? What must be done to return to the right or-
    der and balance of the verbs *to be* and *to do* in Christ?
    Contemplate these questions for your own walk of
    faith and also for your church.

2. "Rightly understood, faith is not a substitute for
    moral conduct but a means toward it." Read James
    2:14–26 about the relation between faith and works.
    Only dynamic faith in God has works that bring glo-
    ry to God. Reflect on the practice of faith and works
    in your life during the past few months. How has it
    been evident?

3. Many local churches have adopted a secular "busi-
    ness model" of getting things done. How is this dif-
    ferent than "showing my faith by my works" and so
    counter to the divine model?

4. Religion is not a substitute for action. In addition, religion should not just produce action but faith-filled action. Think through these distinctions and pray for the Lord to guide you in applying them in your life.

Chapter 14

True Faith Is Active, Not Passive

A Christian is one who believes in Jesus Christ as Lord. With this statement every evangelical agrees. Indeed there would appear to be nothing else to do, because the New Testament is crystal clear about the matter.

This first acknowledgment of Christ as Lord and Savior is usually followed by baptism and membership in a Protestant church, the one because it satisfies a craving for fellowship with others of like mind. A few Christians shy away from organized religion, but the vast majority, while they recognize the imperfections of the churches, nevertheless feel that they can serve their Lord better in the church than out of it.

There is, however, one serious flaw in all this: It

is that many—would I overstate the case if I said the majority?—of those who confess their faith in Christ and enter into association with the community of believers have little joy in their hearts, no peace in their minds and from all external appearances are no better morally than the ordinary educated citizen who takes no interest whatever in religion and, of course, makes no profession of Christianity. Why is this?

I believe it is the result of an inadequate concept of Christianity and an imperfect understanding of the revolutionary character of Christian discipleship. Certainly there is nothing new in my conclusion. The evangelists are loud in their lamentation over the bodies of dead church members, as well they might be, and many thoughtful articles and books appear from time to time dealing with the serious hiatus between faith and practice among Christians.

Why then add another feeble voice to the many? Because many who lament the condition do not seem to know what to do about it, and because I believe that the way is plain, if hard; and that there is no excuse for going on at this poor dying rate when we can enjoy abundant life in Christ Jesus. True faith brings a spiritual and moral transformation and an inward witness that cannot be mistaken. These come when we stop believing in belief and start believing in the Lord Jesus Christ indeed.

True faith is not passive but active. It requires

that we meet certain conditions, that we allow the teachings of Christ to dominate our total lives from the moment we believe. The man of saving faith must be willing to be different from others. The effort to enjoy the benefits of redemption while enmeshed in the world is futile. We must choose one or the other; and faith quickly makes its choice, one from which there is no retreat.

The change experienced by a truly converted man is equal to that of a man moving to another country. The regenerated soul feels no more at home in the world than Abraham felt when he left Ur of the Chaldees and set out for the land of promise. Apart from his own small company he was a stranger to everyone around him. He was called "Abraham the Hebrew," and if he spoke the language of the people among whom he took up his dwelling place, he spoke it with an accent. They all knew that he was not one of them.

This journey from Ur to Bethel is taken by every soul that sets out to follow Christ. It is, however, not a journey for the feet but for the heart. The newborn Christian is a migrant; he has come into the kingdom of God from his old home in the kingdom of man and he must get set for the violent changes that will inevitably follow.

One of the first changes will be a shift of interest from earth to heaven, from men to God, from time to eternity, from earthly gain to Christ and His eternal kingdom. Suddenly, or slowly but surely, he

will develop a new pattern of life. Old things will
pass away and behold, all things will become new
(see 2 Corinthians 5:17), first inwardly and then
outwardly; for the change within him will soon begin to express itself by corresponding changes in
his manner of living.

The transformation will show itself in many
ways and his former friends will begin to worry
about him. At first they will tease him and then
chide him; and if he persists in his determination to
follow Christ, they may begin to oppose and per-
secute. The once-born never understand the twice-
born, and still after thousands of years, Cain hates
Abel and Esau threatens Jacob. It is as true today
as it was in Bible times that the man who hates his
sins too much will get into trouble with those who
do not hate sin enough. People resent having their
friends turn away from them and by implication
condemn their way of life.

The change will reveal itself further in what the
new Christian reads, in the places he goes and the
friends he cultivates, what he does with his time
and how he spends his money. Indeed faith leaves
no area of the new believer's life unaffected.

The genuinely renewed man will have a new life
center. He will experience a new orientation affect-
ing his whole personality. He will become aware
of a different philosophic outlook. Things he once
held to be of value may suddenly lose all their at-
traction for him and he may even hate some things

he formerly loved.

The man who recoils from this revolutionary kind of Christianity is retreating before the cross. But thousands do so retreat, and they try to make things right by seeking baptism and church membership. No wonder they are so dissatisfied.

Questions for Reflection
True Faith Is Active, Not Passive

1. "True faith brings a spiritual and moral transfor-
    mation and an inward witness that cannot be mis-
    taken. These come when we stop believing in belief
    and start believing in the Lord Jesus Christ indeed."
    What aspects of your faith are visible at home, in
    your community, at your job, in your recreation and
    free time? Are the teachings of Christ dominating
    your total life in all areas? If there is an arena where
    your faith is not visible or watered down, discuss
    with a spiritual mentor what changes you need
    to make—in God's way, with God's power and in
    God's time.

2. For new believers, the change from the old life to
    the new life in Christ is a radical shift of focus from
    earth to heaven, from men to God, from time to eter-
    nity and from earthly gain to Christ and His king-
    dom. During time, however, some believers leave
    their first love (Revelation 2:4) and their faith in God
    seriously declines. What causes a person to leave his
    or her first love? How can this decline be reversed?

3. Tozer notes that true "faith leaves no area of the new
    believer's life unaffected." The books and maga-
    zines he reads, the television shows he watches, the
    friendships he cultivates, the discretionary use of his

money, his political views—there are no "hands-off" areas to God! Think about your own life—are there any areas you have not released to God and allowed Him to transform? If so, acknowledge them to God and release them into His hands.

4. Tozer tells us that those who recoil from a revolutionary, active faith in Christ are "retreating from the cross." This leads to dissatisfaction and a crippled faith. For someone who has retreated from the cross, what is the first step to the restoration of a dynamic faith? What are the next steps?

Chapter 15

Faith: The Misunderstood Doctrine

In the divine scheme of salvation the doctrine of faith is central. God addresses His words to faith, and where no faith is, no true revelation is possible. "Without faith it is impossible to please him" (Hebrews 11:6).

Every benefit flowing from the atonement of Christ comes to the individual through the gateway of faith. Forgiveness, cleansing, regeneration, the Holy Spirit, all answers to prayer are given to faith and received by faith. There is no other way. This is common evangelical doctrine and is accepted wherever the cross of Christ is understood.

Because faith is so vital to all our hopes, so necessary to the fulfillment of our hearts, we dare take nothing for granted concerning it. Anything that carries with it so much of weal or woe, which indeed decides our heaven or our hell, is too important to neglect. We simply must not allow ourselves to be uninformed or misinformed. We must know.

For a number of years my heart has been troubled over the doctrine of faith as it is received and taught among evangelical Christians everywhere. Great emphasis is laid upon faith in orthodox circles, and that is good; but still I am troubled. Specifically, my fear is that the modern conception of faith is not the biblical one; that when the teachers of our day use the word they do not mean what Bible writers meant when they used it.

The causes of my uneasiness are these:

1. The lack of spiritual fruit in the lives of so many who claim to have faith.

2. The rarity of a radical change in the conduct and general outlook of persons professing their new faith in Christ as their personal Savior.

3. The failure of teachers to define or even describe the thing to which the word *faith* is supposed to refer.

4. The heartbreaking failure of multitudes of seekers, be they ever so earnest, to make anything out of the doctrine or to receive any satisfying experience through it.

5. The real danger that a doctrine that is par-

roted so widely and received so uncritically by so many is false as understood by them.

6. I have seen faith put forward as a substitute for obedience, an escape from reality, a refuge from the necessity of hard thinking, a hiding place for weak character. I have known people to miscall by the name of faith high animal spirits, natural optimism, emotional thrills and nervous tics.

7. Plain horse sense ought to tell us that anything that makes no change in the man who professes it makes no difference to God either, and it is an easily observable fact that for countless numbers of persons the change from no faith to faith makes no actual difference in life.

Perhaps it will help us to know what faith is if we first notice what it is not. It is not the believing of a statement we know to be true. The human mind is so constructed that it must of necessity believe when the evidence presented to it is convincing. It cannot help itself. When the evidence fails to convince, no faith is possible. No threats, no punishment can compel the mind to believe against clear evidence.

Faith based upon reason is faith of a kind, it is true; *but it is not of the character of Bible faith,* for it follows the evidence infallibly and has nothing of a moral or spiritual nature in it. Neither can the absence of faith based upon reason be held against anyone, for the evidence, not the individual, decides the verdict. To send a man to hell whose only crime was to follow evidence straight to its proper conclusion would be palpable injustice; to justify a sinner on the grounds that he had made up his mind according to the plain facts would be to make salvation the result of workings of a common law of the mind as applicable to Judas as to Paul. It would take salvation out of the realm of the volitional and place it in the mental, where according to the Scriptures, it surely does not belong.

True faith rests upon the character of God and asks no further proof than the moral perfections of the One who cannot lie. It is enough that God said it, and if the statement should contradict every one of the five senses and all the conclusions of logic as well, still the believer continues to believe. "Let God be true, but every man a liar" (Romans 3:4), is the language of true faith. Heaven approves such faith because it rises above mere proofs and rests in the bosom of God.

In recent years among certain evangelicals there has arisen a movement designed to prove the truths of Scriptures by appeal to science. Evidence is sought in the natural world to support supernatural revelation. Snowflakes, blood, stones, strange marine creatures, birds and many other natural objects are brought forward as proof that the Bible is true. This is touted as being a great support to faith, the idea being that if a Bible doctrine can be *proved* to be true, faith will spring up and flourish as a consequence.

What these brethren do not see is that the very fact that they feel a necessity to seek proof for the truths of the Scriptures proves something else altogether, namely, their own basic unbelief. When God speaks, unbelief asks, "How shall I know that this is true?" I AM THAT I AM is the only grounds for faith. To dig among the rocks or search under the sea for evidence to support Scriptures is to insult the One who wrote them. Certainly I do not believe that this is done intentionally; but I cannot see how we can escape the conclusion that it is done, nevertheless.

Faith as the Bible knows it is confidence in God and His Son Jesus Christ; it is the response of the soul to the divine character as revealed in the Scriptures; and even this response is impossible apart from the prior inworking of the Holy Spirit. Faith is a gift of God to a penitent soul and has nothing whatsoever to do with the senses or the data they afford. Faith is a miracle; it is the ability God gives to trust His Son, and anything that does not result in action in accord with the will of God is not faith but something else short of it.

Faith and morals are two sides of the same coin. Indeed the very essence of faith is moral. Any professed faith in Christ as personal Savior that does not bring the life under plenary obedience to Christ as Lord is inadequate and must betray its victim at the last.

The man who believes will obey; failure to obey is convincing proof that there is not true faith present. To attempt the impossible, God must give faith or there will be none, and He gives faith to the obedient heart only. Where real repentance is, there is obedience; for repentance is not only sorrow for past failures and sins, it is a determination to begin now to do the will of God as He reveals it to us.

Questions for Reflection
Faith: The Misunderstood Doctrine

1. "Every benefit flowing from the atonement of Christ comes to the individual through the gateway of faith. Forgiveness, cleansing, regeneration, the Holy Spirit, all answers to prayer are given to faith and received by faith." That is why the story of the ten lepers (Luke 17:11–19) who come to Jesus seeking mercy is so critical for believers today. Nine went away happy with the physical benefits that they got from Jesus, but one leper came back glorifying God, thanking Him, and worshipping the Benefactor of all. He was commended for his faith! What has been your focus over the past few months—the benefits of your salvation or knowing your divine Benefactor better? Spend some time thinking about the differences between these two contrasting focuses.

2. Tozer states seven reasons for the modern conception of faith not being the biblical one. "The lack of spiritual fruit in the lives of so many who claim to have faith" is the first reason. A typical explanation for a lack of spiritual fruit is that the person is not a true believer. Another is that sin or life's trials have derailed a normally fruitful believer. A third possibility is that there is some spiritual fruit, but there should be more. Why is it so critical to assess spiritual fruit? Choose another one of the reasons and reflect on it.

3. "True faith rests upon the character of God and asks no further proof than the moral perfections of the One who cannot lie." If what God said contradicts every one of the five senses and all the conclusions of logic as well, the believer with true faith continues to believe. How does a believer develop a deep understanding of God's character to enable him to have this kind of faith?

4. A faith response to the divine character of God as revealed in the Scriptures is "impossible apart from the prior inworking of the Holy Spirit." Reflect on this statement as it relates to the importance of the Holy Spirit for daily walking by faith.

5. Faith and obedience are connected in the Scriptures. "Without faith it is impossible to please Him" (Hebrews 11:6). Go through Hebrews 11 and note the instances of faith and obedience. Now, take some time to meditate on your faith and obedience during the past several weeks. Pray back to God your findings and ask God for His solutions.

Chapter 16

Are We Evangelicals Social Climbing?

Traditionally Christianity has been the religion of the common people. Whenever the upper classes have adopted it in numbers, it has died. Respectability has almost always proved fatal to it.

The reasons back of this are two: one human and the other divine.

Schleiermacher has pointed out that at the bottom of all religion there lies a feeling of dependence, a sense of creature helplessness. The simple man who lives close to the earth lives also close to death and knows that he must look for help beyond himself; he knows that there is but a step between him and catastrophe. As he rises in the social and economic scale, he surrounds himself with more and more protective devices and pushes danger (so he thinks) farther and farther from him. Self-confidence displaces the feeling of dependence he once knew and God becomes less necessary to him. Should he stop to think this through, he would know better than to place his confidence in things and people; but so badly are we injured by our moral fall that we are capable of deceiving ourselves completely and, if conditions favor it, to keep up the deception for a lifetime.

Along with the feeling of security that wealth and position bring comes an arrogant pride that shuts tightly the door of the heart to the waiting Savior. Our Very Important Man may indeed honor a church by joining it, but there is no life in his act. His religion is external and his faith nominal. Conscious respectability has destroyed him.

The second reason Christianity tends to decline as its devotees move up the social scale is that God will not respect persons nor share His glory with another. Paul sets this forth plainly enough in his First Corinthians epistle:

Because the foolishness of God is wiser than men; and the weakness of God is stronger than men. For ye see your calling, brethren, how that not many wise men after the flesh, not many mighty, not many noble, are called: But God hath chosen the foolish things of the world to confound the wise; and God hath chosen the weak things of the world to confound the things which are mighty; and base things of the world, and things which are despised, hath God chosen, yea, and things which are not, to bring to nought things that are: That no flesh should glory in his presence. (1 Corinthians 1:25–29)

When God sent His Son to redeem mankind, He sent Him to the home of a working man and He grew up to be what we now call a peasant. When He presented Himself to Israel and launched into His earthly ministry, He was rejected by the respectable religionists and had to look for followers almost exclusively from among the poor, plain people. When the Spirit came and the church was founded, its first members were the socially unacceptable. For generations the church drew her numbers from among the lower classes, individual exceptions occurring now and again, of which Saul of Tarsus was the most noteworthy.

During the centuries since Pentecost, the path of true Christianity has paralleled pretty closely the path Jesus walked when He was here on earth: It was to be rejected by the great and accepted by the lowly. The institutionalized church has certainly not been poor, nor has she lacked for great and mighty men to swell her membership. But this great church has had no power. Almost always the approval of God has rested upon small and marginal groups whose members were scorned while they lived and managed to gain acceptance only after they had been safely dead several score years.

Today we evangelicals are showing signs that we are becoming too rich and too prominent for our own good. With a curious disregard for the lessons of history, we are busy fighting for recognition by the world and acceptance by society. And we are winning both. The great and the mighty are now looking our way. The world seems about to come over and join us. Of course we must make some concessions, but these have almost all been made already except for a bit of compromising here and there on such matters as verbal inspiration, special creation, separation and religious tolerance.

Evangelical Christianity is fast becoming the religion of the bourgeoisie. The well-to-do, the upper middle classes, the politically prominent, the celebrities are accepting our religion by the thousands and parking their expensive cars outside our church doors, to the uncontrollable glee of our religious leaders who seem completely blind to the fact that the vast majority of these new patrons of the Lord of glory have not altered their moral habits in the slightest nor given any evidence of true conversion that would have been accepted by the saintly fathers who built the churches.

Yes, history is a great teacher, but she cannot teach those who do not want to learn. And apparently we do not.

Questions for Reflection
Are We Evangelicals Social Climbing?

1. "The simple man who lives close to the earth lives also close to death and knows that he must look for help beyond himself; he knows that there is but a step between him and catastrophe. As he rises in the social and economic scale, he surrounds himself with more and more protective devices and pushes danger (so he thinks) farther and farther from him." What are some of the "protective devices" that Tozer speaks of? What are some of your protective devices? How do they tend to undermine faith in God?

2. There is a destructive spiraling impact of placing confidence in things and people. For instance, trust in wealth and position leads to an arrogance that "shuts tightly the door of the heart to the waiting Savior." How does one break the bondage of this self-deception? List some practical steps to freedom from dependence on things and people.

3. During Tozer's day, he saw that evangelical Christianity was fast becoming the religion of the bourgeoisie and not that of the socially unacceptable as in the early church. How do you see evangelical Christianity today? If what you see undermines faith in God, what can you personally do?

4. "The institutionalized church has certainly not been poor, nor has she lacked for great and mighty men to swell her membership. But this great church has had no power." What are the signs of a powerless church? What can individuals do to counteract powerlessness in the church?

5. Are the church and individual believers fighting for recognition by the world and acceptance by society today? Or is there an accelerated hostility from the world and society? Regardless of the reality in our corner of the world, what must we continue to do?

Chapter 17

Faith without Expectation Is Dead

Expectation and faith, though alike, are not identical. An instructed Christian will not confuse the two.

True faith is never found alone; it is always accompanied by expectation. The man who believes the promises of God expects to see them fulfilled. Where there is no expectation, there is no faith.

It is, however, quite possible for expectation to be present where no faith is. The mind is quite capable of mistaking strong desire for faith. Indeed faith, as commonly understood, is little more than desire compounded with cheerful optimism. Certain writers make a comfortable living promoting that kind of so-called faith, which is supposed to create the "positive" as opposed to the negative mind. Their effusions are dear to the hearts of those in the population who are afflicted with a psychological compulsion to believe, and who manage to live with facts only by the simple expedient of ignoring them.

Real faith is not the stuff dreams are made of; rather it is tough, practical and altogether realistic. Faith sees the invisible but it does not see the non-existent. Faith engages God, the one great Reality, who gave and gives existence to all things. God's promises conform to reality, and whoever trusts them enters a world not of fiction but of fact.

In common experience we arrive at truth by observation. Whatever can be verified by experiment is accepted as true. Men believe the report of their senses. If it walks like a duck, looks like a duck and quacks like a duck, it is probably a duck. And if its eggs hatch into little ducks, the test is about complete. Probability gives way to certainty; it is a duck. This is a valid way to deal with our environment. No one dare complain about it for everyone does it. It is the way we manage to get on in this world.

But faith introduces another and radically different element into our lives. "By faith we know" is the word that lifts our knowing onto a higher level. Faith engages facts that have been revealed from heaven and by their nature they do not respond to scientific tests. The Christian knows a thing to be true, not because he has verified it in experience but because God has said it. His expectations spring from his confidence in the character of God.

Expectation has always been present in the church in the times of her greatest power. When she believed, she expected, and her Lord never disappointed her. "And blessed is she that believed: for there shall be a performance of those things which were told her from the Lord" (Luke 1:45).

Every great movement of God in history, every unusual advance in the church, every revival, has been preceded by a sense of keen anticipation. Expectation accompanied the operations of the Spirit always. His bestowals hardly surprised His people because they were gazing expectantly toward the risen Lord and looking confidently for His Word to be fulfilled. His blessings accorded with their expectations.

One characteristic that marks the average church today is lack of anticipation. Christians when they meet do not expect anything unusual to happen; consequently only the usual happens, and that usual is as predictable as the setting of the sun. A psychology of nonexpectation pervades the assembly, a mood of quiet ennui that the minister by various means tries to dispel, the means depending upon the cultural level of the congregation and particularly of the minister.

One will resort to humor, another will latch on to some topic currently dividing the public, such as fluoridation, capital punishment or Sunday sports.

Another who may have a modest opinion of his gifts as a humorist and who is not sure which side of a controversy he may safely support will seek to arouse expectation by outlining enthusiastically the shape of things to come: the men's banquet to be held at the Chicken-in-a-Basket Tea Room next Thursday evening; or the picnic with its thrilling game to be played between the married men and the single men, the outcome of which the jocular minister coyly refuses to predict; or the coming premier of the new religious film, full of sex, violence and false philosophy but candied over with vapid moralizings and gentle suggestions that the enraptured viewers should be born again.

The activities of the saints are thus laid out for them by those who are supposed to know what they need better than they do. And this planned play is made acceptable to the more pious-minded by tagging on a few words of devotion at the close. This is called "fellowship," though it bears scant resemblance to the activities of those Christians to which the word was first applied.

Christian expectation in the average church follows the program, not the promises. Prevailing spiritual conditions, however low, are accepted as inevitable. What will be is what has been. The weary slaves of the dull routine find it impossible to hope for anything better.

We need today a fresh spirit of anticipation that springs out of the promises of God. We must declare war on the mood of nonexpectation and come together with childlike faith. Only then can we know again the beauty and wonder of the Lord's presence among us.

Questions for Reflection
Faith without Expectation Is Dead

1. "True faith is never found alone; it is always accompanied by expectation." However, there can be expectation but no faith. If one is standing by faith on the promises of God or on the character of God behind the promises, then there should be expectation that God will answer and act accordingly. What things tend to undermine faith-filled expectation? Make a list of them, and reflect on one of them. What changes must be made to avoid the undermining of expectation?

2. "Faith sees the invisible but it does not see the nonexistent. Faith engages God, the one great Reality, who gave and gives existence to all things." Rate the level of your engagement with God this past week on a 1 to 10 scale. What could you have done differently this past week to have increased your rating?

3. The Christian's "expectations should spring from his confidence in the character of God." How can we bolster our confidence in the character of God? Act on your answer to this question by implementing it in your own life.

4. "Christian expectation in the average church follows the program, not the promises." If this is the tendency in a church, what can be done to protect the faith of the believers in that church?

5. "We need today a fresh spirit of anticipation that springs out of the promises of God. We must declare war on the mood of nonexpectation and come together with childlike faith. Only then can we know again the beauty and the wonder of the Lord's presence among us." Reflect on the depths and implications of this Tozer quote to you and to your portrayal of Christ to others.

Chapter 18

Why People
Find the Bible Difficult

That many persons find the Bible hard to understand will not be denied by those acquainted with the facts. Testimony to the difficulties encountered in Bible reading is too full and too widespread to be dismissed lightly.

In human experience there is usually a complex of causes rather than but one cause for everything, and so it is with the difficulty we run into with the Bible. To the question, Why is the Bible hard to understand? no snap answer can be given; the pert answer is sure to be the wrong one. The problem is multiple instead of singular, and for this reason the efforts to find a single solution to it will be disappointing.

In spite of this I venture to give a short answer to

the question, and while it is not the whole answer it is a major one and probably contains within itself most of the answers to what must be an involved and highly complex question. *I believe that we find the Bible difficult because we try to read it as we would read any other book, and it is not the same as any other book.*

The Bible is not addressed to just anybody. Its message is directed to a chosen few. Whether these few are chosen by God in a sovereign act of election or are chosen because they meet certain qualifying conditions, I leave to each one to decide as he may, knowing full well that his decision will be determined by his basic beliefs about such matters as predestination, free will, the eternal decrees and other related doctrines. But whatever may have taken place in eternity, it is obvious what happens in time: Some believe and some do not. It is to those who do and are and have that the Bible is addressed. Those who do not and are not and have not will read it in vain.

Right here I expect some readers to enter strenuous objections, and for reasons not hard to find. Christianity today is man-centered, not God-centered. God is made to wait patiently, even respectfully, on the whims of men. The image of God currently popular is that of a distracted Father, struggling in heartbroken desperation to get people to accept a Savior of whom they feel no need and in whom they have very little interest. To persuade

these self-sufficient souls to respond to His gener-
ous offers, God will do almost anything, even using
salesmanship methods and talking down to them
in the chummiest way imaginable. This view of
things is, of course, a kind of religious romanticism
that, while it often uses flattering and sometimes
embarrassing terms in praise of God, manages nevertheless to make man the star of the show.

The notion that the Bible is addressed to everybody has wrought confusion within and without
the church. The effort to apply the teaching of the
Sermon on the Mount to the unregenerate nations
of the world is one example of this. Courts of law
and the military powers of the earth are urged to
follow the teachings of Christ, an obviously impossible thing for them to do. To quote the words of
Christ as guides for policemen, judges and generals
is to misunderstand those words completely and to
reveal a total lack of understanding of the purposes
of divine revelation. The gracious words of Christ
are for the sons and daughters of grace, not for the
Gentile nations whose chosen symbols are the lion,
the eagle, the dragon and the bear.

Not only does God address His words of truth
to those who are able to receive them, He actually
conceals their meaning from those who are not.
The preacher uses stories to make truth clear; our
Lord often used them to obscure it. The parables of
Christ were the exact opposite to the modern "illustration," which is meant to give light; the parables

were "dark sayings," and Christ asserted that He sometimes used them so that His disciples could understand and His enemies could not. (See Matthew 13:10–17.) As the pillar of fire gave light to Israel but was cloud and darkness to the Egyptians, so our Lord's words shine in the hearts of His people but leave the self-confident unbeliever in the obscurity of moral night.

The saving power of the Word is reserved for those for whom it is intended. The secret of the Lord is with them who fear Him. The impenitent heart will find the Bible but a skeleton of facts without flesh or life or breath. Shakespeare may be enjoyed without penitence; we may understand Plato without believing a word he says; but penitence and humility along with faith and obedience are necessary to a right understanding of the Scriptures.

In natural matters faith follows evidence and is impossible without it, but in the realm of the spirit, faith precedes understanding; it does not follow it. The natural man must know in order to believe; the spiritual man must believe in order to know. The faith that saves is not a conclusion drawn from evidence; it is a moral thing of the spirit, a supernatural infusion of confidence in Jesus Christ, a very gift of God.

The faith that saves reposes in the person of Christ; it leads at once to a committal of the total being to Christ, an act impossible to the natural man. To believe rightly is as much a miracle as was the coming forth of dead Lazarus at the command of Christ.

The Bible is a supernatural book and can be understood only by supernatural aid.

Questions for Reflection
Why People Find the Bible Difficult

1. "The Bible is a supernatural book and can be understood only by supernatural aid." In light of this truth, it is obvious that we should not read it like it was just another book. How should the Bible be read? It is very, very likely that those who read the Bible with supernatural help have a greater faith in God. Why is that?

2. If the Bible is a supernatural book, understood only with supernatural aid, it seems apparent that spending five minutes alone with God or ten minutes reading a commentary about a passage would be inadequate to building our faith in Him. What is the short-term and long-term process for developing a greater understanding of biblical truth?

3. "Christianity today is man-centered, not God-centered." How does a man-centered perspective affect one's reading and understanding of the Bible or just hearing God's voice? Because this man-centered Christianity deafens our ears to the voice of God and thus forces God to shout louder, what is the divine solution to this man-centered Christianity? How does this man-centered perspective affect our daily walk with Him? Reflect on the central focus of your own Bible study and daily walk during the past year.

4. "Penitence and humility along with faith and obedience are necessary to a right understanding of the Scriptures." Has there been a time in your life where your understanding of the Scriptures was greater than now? What was your walk of faith in Christ like at that time?

5. "In the realm of the spirit, faith precedes understanding; it does not follow it. The natural man must know in order to believe; the spiritual man must believe in order to know." If, as Tozer says, faith is necessary to understanding the Scriptures, how can a believer be sure that he is reading the Bible by faith?

REALITIES OF FAITH

Chapter 19

Let's Cultivate Simplicity and Solitude

We Christians must simplify our lives or lose untold treasures on earth and in eternity.

Modern civilization is so complex as to make the devotional life all but impossible. It wears us out by multiplying distractions and beats us down by destroying our solitude, where otherwise we might drink and renew our strength before going out to face the world again.

"The thoughtful soul to solitude retires," said the poet of other and quieter times; but where is the solitude to which we can retire today? Science, which has provided men with certain material comforts, has robbed them of their souls by surrounding them with a world hostile to their existence. "Commune with your own heart upon your bed, and be still" (Psalm 4:4) is a wise and healing counsel, but how can it be followed in this day of the newspaper, the telephone, the radio and the television? These modern playthings, like pet tiger cubs, have grown so large and dangerous that they threaten to devour us all. What was intended to be a blessing has become a positive curse. No spot is now safe from the world's intrusion.

One way the civilized world destroys men is by preventing them from thinking their own thoughts. Our "vastly improved methods of communication," of which the shortsighted boast so loudly, now enable a few men in strategic centers to feed into millions of minds alien thought stuff, ready-made and predigested. A little effortless assimilation of these borrowed ideas and the average man has done all the thinking he will or can do. This subtle brainwashing goes on day after day and year after year to the eternal injury of the populace—a populace, incidentally, that is willing to pay big money to have the job done, the reason being, I suppose, that it relieves them of the arduous and often frightening task of reaching independent decisions for which they must take responsibility.

There was a time, not too long ago, when a man's home was his castle, a sure retreat to which he might return for quietness and solitude. There "the rains of heaven may blow in but the king himself cannot enter without permission," said the proud British, and made good on their boast. That was home indeed. It was of such a sacred place the poet said:

> O, when I am safe in my sylvan home,
> I tread on the pride of Greece and Rome;
> And when I am stretched beneath the pines,
> Where the evening star so holy shines,
> I laugh at the lore and the pride of man,
> At the sophist schools, and the learned clan;
> For what are they all, in their high conceit,
> When man in the bush with God may meet.
> *Good-bye*
> RALPH WALDO EMERSON

While it is scarcely within the scope of the present piece, I cannot refrain from remarking that the most ominous sign of the coming destruction of our country is the passing of the American home. Americans live no longer in homes, but in theaters. The members of many families hardly know one another, and the face of some popular TV star is to many wives as familiar as that of their husbands. Let no one smile. Rather should we weep at the portent. It will do no good to wrap ourselves in the Stars and Stripes for protection. No nation can long endure whose people have sold themselves for bread and circuses. Our fathers sleep soundly, and the harsh bedlam of commercialized noise that engulfs us like something from Dante's *Inferno* cannot disturb their slumber. They left us a goodly heritage. To preserve that heritage, we must have a national character as strong as theirs. And this can be developed only in the Christian home.

The need for solitude and quietness was never greater than it is today. What the world will do about it is their problem. Apparently the masses want it the way it is, and the majority of Christians are so completely conformed to this present age that they too want things the way they are. They may be annoyed a bit by the clamor and by the goldfish-bowl existence they live, but apparently they are not annoyed enough to do anything about it. However, there are a few of God's children who have had enough. They want to relearn the ways of solitude and simplicity and gain the infinite riches of the interior life. They want to discover the blessedness of what Dr. Max Reich called "spiritual aloneness." To such I offer a brief paragraph of counsel.

Retire from the world each day to some private spot, even if it is only the bedroom (for a while I retreated to the furnace room for want of a better place). Stay in the secret place till the surrounding noises begin to fade out of your heart and a sense of God's presence envelops you. Deliberately tune out the unpleasant sounds and come out of your closet determined not to hear them. Listen for the inward Voice till you learn to recognize it. Stop trying to compete with others. Give yourself to God, and then be what and who you are without regard to what others think. Reduce your interests to a few. Don't try to know what will be of no service to you. Avoid the digest type of mind—short bits of unrelated facts, cute stories and bright sayings. Learn to pray inwardly every moment. After a while you can do this even while you work. Practice candor, childlike honesty, humility. Pray for a single eye. Read less, but read more of what is important to your inner life. Call home your roving thoughts. Gaze on Christ with the eyes of your soul. Practice spiritual concentration. All the above is contingent upon a right relation to God through Christ and daily meditation on the Scriptures. Lacking these, nothing will help us; granted these, the discipline recommended will go far to neutralize the evil effects of externalism and to make us acquainted with God and our own souls.

Questions for Reflection
Let's Cultivate Simplicity and Solitude

1. "Modern civilization is so complex as to make the devotional life all but impossible. It wears us out by multiplying distractions and beats us down by destroying our solitude." Since Tozer's time, the complexity of life has increased all the more through such things as tighter schedules, increased responsibilities and multiplying technology. What are you doing to protect the simplicity and solitude of your time with the Lord? Why are simplicity and solitude so critical to the growth of our faith?

2. To "cease striving [be still, KJV] and know that I am God" (Psalm 46:10) is difficult today with the bombardment of communications media—cell phones, the Internet, e-mail and more. "These modern playthings, like pet tiger cubs, have grown so large and dangerous that they threaten to devour us all. What was intended to be a blessing has become a positive curse." How do we use these blessings to further our relationship with God instead of the blessings using us? What kind of hard decisions must one make to protect his or her walk of faith?

3. "One way the civilized world destroys men is by preventing them from thinking their own thoughts." We tend to assume that messages coming from sev-

eral sources and repeatedly must be right. However, to avoid adopting the world's thoughts, we need to evaluate the truthfulness of the messages we receive and take every thought captive to the obedience of Christ (2 Corinthians 10:5). How does one do this on a day-to-day basis?

4. With all of the fast pace today, there is a tremendous need for solitude and quietness. Tozer notes that "the majority of Christians are so completely conformed to this present age that they too want things the way they are." How does one step away from this conformity to the world on a daily basis? What actions may be necessary to protect our faith in God?

5. Tozer says that believers need to find a place and time where they can tune out the world and all distractions, where they cultivate a quiet atmosphere to hear the Lord as they pray and study the Scriptures, and where they can "gaze on Christ with the eyes of the soul." What do you need to do to nurture and protect this time and place?

Chapter 20

Marks of the Spiritual Man

The concept of spirituality varies among different Christian groups. In some circles the highly vocal person who talks religion continually is thought to be very spiritual; others accept noisy exuberance as a mark of spirituality, and in some churches the man who prays first, longest and loudest gets a reputation for being the most spiritual man in the assembly.

Now a vigorous testimony, frequent prayers and loud praise may be entirely consistent with spirituality, but it is important that we understand that they do not in themselves constitute it nor prove that it is present.

True spirituality manifests itself in certain dominant desires. These are ever-present, deep-settled wants sufficiently powerful to motivate and control the life. For convenience let me number them, though I make no effort to decide the order of their importance.

1. First is the desire to be holy rather than happy. The yearning after happiness found so widely among Christians professing a superior degree of sanctity is sufficient proof that such sanctity is not indeed present. The truly spiritual man knows that God will give abundance of joy after we have become able to receive it without injury to our souls, but he does not demand it at once. John Wesley said of the members of one of the earliest Methodist societies that he doubted that they had been made perfect in love because they came to church to enjoy religion instead of to learn how they could become holy.

2. A man may be considered spiritual when he wants to see the honor of God advanced through his life even if it means that he himself must suffer temporary dishonor or loss. Such a man prays, "Hallowed be Thy name," and silently adds, "at any cost to me, Lord." He lives for God's honor by a kind of spiritual reflex. Every choice involving the glory of God is for him already made before it presents itself. He does not need to debate the matter with his own heart; there is nothing to

debate. The glory of God is necessary to him; he gasps for it as a suffocating man gasps for air.

3. The spiritual man wants to carry his cross. Many Christians accept adversity or tribulation with a sigh and call it their cross, forgetting that such things come alike to saint and sinner. The cross is that extra adversity that comes to us as a result of our obedience to Christ. This cross is not forced upon us; we voluntarily take it up with full knowledge of the consequences. We choose to obey Christ and by so doing choose to carry the cross.

Carrying a cross means to be attached to the person of Christ, committed to the lordship of Christ and obedient to the commandments of Christ. The man who is so attached, so committed, so obedient is a spiritual man.

4. Again, a Christian is spiritual when he sees everything from God's viewpoint. The ability to weigh all things in the divine scale and place the same value upon them as God does is the mark of a Spirit-filled life.

God looks at and through at the same time. His gaze does not rest on the surface but penetrates to the true meaning of things. The carnal Christian looks at an object or a situation, but because he does not see through it, he is elated or cast down by what he sees.

The spiritual man is able to look through things as God looks and think of them as God thinks. He insists on seeing all things as God sees them even if it humbles him and exposes his ignorance to the point of real pain.

5. Another desire of the spiritual man is to die right rather than to live wrong. A sure mark of the mature man of God is his nonchalance about living. The earth-loving, body-conscious Christian looks upon death with numb terror in his heart; but as he goes on to live in the Spirit, he becomes increasingly indifferent to the number of his years here below, and at the same time increasingly careful of the kind of life he lives while he is here. He will not purchase a few extra days of life at the cost of compromise or failure. He wants most of all to be right, and he is happy to let God decide how long he shall live. He knows that he can afford to die now that he is in Christ, but he knows that he cannot afford to do wrong, and this knowledge becomes a gyroscope to stabilize his thinking and his acting.

6. The desire to see others advance at his expense is another mark of the spiritual man. He wants to see other Christians above him and is happy when they are promoted and he is overlooked. There is no envy in his heart;

when his brethren are honored, he is pleased because such is the will of God and that will is his earthly heaven. If God is pleased, he is pleased for that reason, and if it pleases God to exalt another above him, he is content to have it so.

7. The spiritual man habitually makes eternity-judgments instead of time-judgments. By faith he rises above the tug of earth and the flow of time and learns to think and feel as one who has already left the world and gone to join the innumerable company of angels and the general assembly and church of the firstborn, which are written in heaven. Such a man would rather be useful than famous and would rather serve than be served.

And all this must be by the operation of the Holy Spirit within him. No man can become spiritual by himself. Only the free Spirit can make a man spiritual.

Questions for Reflection
Marks of the Spiritual Man

1. One of the marks of the spiritual man is "the desire to be holy rather than happy." What is the nature of the conflict between holiness and happiness for the believer?

2. Another mark of the spiritual man is that "he sees everything from God's viewpoint" and "his gaze does not rest on the surface but penetrates to the true meaning of things." In fact, he insists on seeing all as God sees even if it humbles or breaks him. Why is it that this is only possible when we walk by faith? What spiritual disciplines need to be ingrained in our life to be able to see as God sees?

3. The spiritual man wants to see God glorified in all that he does and desires to see others advance at his expense. This has to be a work of the Holy Spirit in a believer's life. Of course, at times we may want to see God glorified and others advance, but sometimes we may want what we want no matter what. What checks and balances do we need to have in place to quench this selfish attitude?

4. Tozer rightly notes that "no man [or woman] can be-
    come spiritual by himself. Only the free Spirit can
    make a man spiritual." In that light, what does a be-
    liever need to understand about the role of the Word
    of God and the Holy Spirit in the life of faith as well
    as in service to others out of that faith?

5. Frequently, when a believer dies young, his friends
    and family bemoan the fact that he missed living a
    full and vibrant life. However, it is not how long one
    lives that pleases God, but whether they walked by
    faith in the time that they had. For instance, Enoch
    lived only about a third of the life span of his con-
    temporaries (Genesis 5), but he walked with God by
    faith in the time he had and God took him (Hebrews
    11:5). As a result, he died right! Meditate on the tre-
    mendous encouragement from these thoughts and
    Scriptures as a motivation to walk by faith from now
    on.

Chapter 21

The Bible World Is the Real World

W̲hen reading the Scriptures, the sensitive person is sure to feel the marked difference between the world as the Bible reveals it and the world as conceived by religious people today. And the contrast is not in our favor.

The world as the men and women of the Bible saw it was a personal world, warm, intimate, populated. Their world contained first of all the God who had created it, who still dwelt in it as in a sanctuary and who might be discovered walking among the trees of the garden if the human heart were but pure enough to feel and human eyes clear enough to see. And there were also present many beings sent of God to be ministers to them who were the heirs of salvation. They also recognized the presence of sinister forces, which it was their duty to oppose and which they might easily conquer by an appeal to God in prayer.

Christians today think of the world in wholly different terms. Science, which has brought us many benefits, has with them also brought us a world wholly different from that which we see in the Scriptures. Today's world consists of wide and limitless spaces, having here and there at remote distances from each other blind and meaningless bodies controlled only by natural laws from which they can never escape. That world is cold and impersonal and completely without inhabitants except for man, the little shivering ephemeral being that clings to the soil, which he rides "round in earth's diurnal course with rocks and stones and trees" (William Wordsworth, 1798).

How glorious is the world as men of the Bible knew it! Jacob saw a ladder set up on the earth with God standing above it and the angels ascending and descending upon it. Abraham and Balaam and Manoah and how many others met the angels of God and conversed with them. Moses saw God in the bush; Isaiah saw Him high and lifted up and heard the antiphonal chant filling the temple.

Ezekiel saw a great cloud and fire unfolding itself, and out of the midst thereof came the likeness of four living creatures. Angels were present to tell of Jesus' coming birth and to celebrate that birth when it took place in Bethlehem; angels comforted our Lord when He prayed in Gethsemane; angels are mentioned in some of the inspired epistles; and the book of the Revelation is bright with the presence of strange and beautiful creatures intent upon the affairs of earth and heaven.

Yes, the true world is a populated world. The blind eyes of modern Christians cannot see the invisible, but that does not destroy the reality of the spiritual creation. Unbelief has taken from us the comfort of a personal world. We have accepted the empty and meaningless world of science as the true one, forgetting that science is valid only when dealing with material things and can know nothing about God and the spiritual world.

We must have faith; and let us not apologize for it, for faith is an organ of knowledge and can tell us more about ultimate reality than all the findings of science. We are not opposed to science, but we recognize its proper limitations and refuse to stop where it is compelled to stop. The Bible tells of another world too fine for the instruments of scientific research to discover. By faith we engage that world and make it ours. It is accessible to us through the blood of the everlasting covenant. If we will believe, we may even now enjoy the presence of God and the ministry of His heavenly messengers. Only unbelief can rob us of this royal privilege.

Questions for Reflection
The Bible World Is the Real World

1. "The world as men and women of the Bible saw it was a personal world, warm, intimate, populated" by God, angels and sinister forces. Today's world, permeated by the blessings and curses of science, is cold and impersonal, with man at the center and God ignored or denied. "The blind eyes of modern Christians cannot see the invisible but that does not destroy the reality of the spiritual creation. Unbelief has taken from us the comfort of a personal world." Do you see the personal world that the men and women of the Bible saw? What is the secret to seeing the spiritual world? What is God's part and what is your part?

2. "Science is valid only when dealing with material things and can know nothing about God and the spiritual world." Do you agree or disagree with this statement? If you disagree, why? If you agree, where is the place of science and our faith?

3. "Faith is an organ of knowledge and can tell us more about ultimate reality than all the findings of science." What kind of knowledge is Tozer talking about? What does he mean by "ultimate reality"?

4. "By faith we engage that world and make it ours." Reflect on the depths of this comment by Tozer. Later, Tozer says that only unbelief can rob us of the royal privileges granted to us by God in this world. Have you ever experienced this robbery for a period of time? If so, how did God restore you to the royal position and its privileges?

Chapter 22

In the Praise of Disbelief

In our constant struggle to believe, we are likely to overlook the simple fact that a bit of healthy disbelief is sometimes as needful as faith to the welfare of our souls.

I would go further and say that we would do well to cultivate a reverent skepticism. It will keep us out of a thousand bogs and quagmires where others who lack it sometimes find themselves. It is no sin to doubt some things, but it may be fatal to believe everything.

Faith is at the root of all true worship, and "without faith it is impossible to please [God]" (Hebrews 11:6). Through unbelief it is impossible to please God. Through unbelief Israel failed to inherit the promises. "By grace are ye saved through faith"

(Ephesians 2:8). "The just shall live by faith" (Romans 1:17). Such verses as these come trooping to our memories, and we wince just a little at the suggestion that unbelief may also be a good and useful thing. It sounds like a bold cancellation of the doctrine of faith as taught in the Scriptures and disposes us to write off the brazen advocate of disbelief as a modernist. Let's look at the matter a bit more closely.

Faith never means gullibility. The man who believes everything is as far from God as the man who refuses to believe anything. Faith engages the person and promises of God and rests upon them with perfect assurance. Whatever has behind it the character and word of the living God is accepted by faith as the last and final truth from which there must never be any appeal. Faith never asks questions when it has been established that God has spoken. "Yea, let God be true, but every man a liar" (Romans 3:4). Thus, faith honors God by counting Him righteous and accepts His testimony against the very evidence of its own senses. That is faith, and of such we can never have too much.

Credulity, on the other hand, never honors God, for it shows as great a readiness to believe anybody as to believe God Himself. The credulous person will accept anything as long as it is unusual, and the more unusual it is, the more ardently he will believe. Any testimony will be swallowed with a straight face if it only has about it some element of the eerie, the preternatural, the unearthly. The gullible mentality is like the ostrich that will gulp down anything that looks interesting—an orange, a tennis ball, a pocketknife opened or closed, a paperweight or a ripe apple.

That he survives at all is testimony not to his intelligence but to his tough constitution.

I have met Christians with no more discrimination than the ostrich. Because they must believe certain things, they feel that they must believe everything. Because they are called upon to accept the invisible, they go right on to accept the incredible. God can and does work miracles; ergo, everything that passes for a miracle must be of God. God has spoken to men; therefore, every man who claims to have had a revelation from God must be accepted as a prophet. Whatever is unearthly must be heavenly; whatever cannot be explained must be received as divine; the prophets were rejected; therefore, anyone who is rejected is a prophet; the saints were misunderstood, so everyone who is misunderstood is a saint. This is the dangerous logic of the gullible Christian. And it can be as injurious as unbelief itself.

The healthy soul, like the healthy bloodstream, has its proper proportion of white and red cells. The red corpuscles are like faith: They carry the life-giving oxygen to every part of the body. The white cells are like disbelief: They pounce upon dead and toxic matter and carry it out to the drain. Thus the two kinds of cells working together keep the tissues in good condition. In the healthy heart there must be provision for keeping dead and poisonous matter out of the life stream. This the credulous person never suspects. He is all for faith. He accents the affirmative and cultivates religious optimism to a point where he can no longer tell when he is being imposed upon.

Along with our faith in God must go a healthy disbelief of everything occultic and esoteric. Numerology, astrology, spiritism and everything weird and strange that passes for religion must be rejected. All this is toxic matter and has no place in the life of a true Christian. He will reject the whole business without compunction or fear. He has Christ, and He is the way, the truth and the life. What more does the Christian need?

Questions for Reflection
In the Praise of Disbelief

1. "Faith engages the person and promises of God and rests upon them with perfect assurance." What promises of God have you been clinging to lately? Do you see your faith in God digressing, stagnant or neutral, or progressing? Reflect on the relationship between your view of God's character and your trust in His promises.

2. "Faith never means gullibility. The man who believes everything is as far from God as the man who refuses to believe anything." Why are these two extremes at odds with faith in God? How would you respond to a friend who is very gullible?

3. "Faith never asks questions when it has been established that God has spoken." List some things that God has spoken to you about and your response to that divine voice. Has there been conflict or assent? What has been the impact on your faith in God?

4. "Along with our faith in God must go a healthy disbelief of everything occult and esoteric." We have

Christ, and He is the way, and the truth, and the life (John 14:6). It is easy for our minds to "be led astray from the simplicity and purity of devotion to Christ" (2 Corinthians 11:3). Assess the level of your simplicity and purity of devotion to Christ.

Chapter 23

To Be or to Do

Historically the West has tended to throw its chief emphasis upon doing and the East upon being. What we *are* has always seemed more important to the Oriental; the Occidental has been willing to settle for what we *do*. One has glorified the verb *to be*; the other, the verb *to do*.

Were human nature perfect, there would be no discrepancy between being and doing. The unfallen man would simply live from within, without giving it a thought. His actions would be the true expression of his inner being.

With human nature what it is, however, things are not so simple. Sin has introduced moral confusion and life has become involved and difficult. Those elements within us that were meant to work together in unconscious harmony are often isolated from each other wholly or in part and tend to become actually hostile to each other. For this reason symmetry of character is extremely difficult to achieve.

Out of deep inner confusion arises the antagonism between being and doing, and the verb upon which we throw our emphasis puts us in one of the two categories: We are *be-ers* or we are *do-ers*, one or the other. In our modern civilized society the stress falls almost wholly upon doing.

We Christians cannot escape this question. We must discover where God throws the stress and come around to the divine pattern. And this should not be too difficult since we have before us the sacred Scriptures with all their wealth of spiritual instruction, and to interpret those Scriptures we have the very Spirit who inspired them.

In spite of all our opportunity to know the truth, most of us are still slow to learn. The tendency to accept without question and follow without knowing why is very strong in us. For this reason whatever the majority of Christians hold at any given time is sure to be accepted as true and right beyond a doubt. It is easier to imitate than to originate; it is easier and, for the time being, safer to fall into step without asking too many questions about where the parade is headed.

This is why being has ceased to have much appeal for people and doing engages almost everyone's attention. Modern Christians lack symmetry. They know almost nothing about the inner life. They are like a temple that is all exterior without any interior. Color, light, sound, appearance, motion—these are thy gods, O Israel.

"The accent in the Church today," says Leonard Ravenhill, the English evangelist, "is not on devotion, but on commotion." Religious extroversion has been carried to such an extreme in evangelical circles that hardly anyone has the desire, to say nothing of the courage, to question the soundness of it. Externalism has taken over. God now speaks by the wind and the earthquake only; the still, small voice can be heard no more. The whole religious machine has become a noisemaker. The adolescent taste that loves the loud horn and the thundering exhaust has gotten into the activities of modern Christians. The old question, "What is the chief end of man?" is now answered. "To dash about the world and add to the din thereof." And all this is done in the name of Him who did not strive nor cry nor make His voice to be heard in the streets (see Matthew 12:18–21).

We must begin the needed reform by challenging the spiritual validity of externalism. What a man is must be shown to be more important than what he does. While the moral quality of any act is imparted by the condition of the heart, there may be a world of religious activity that arises not from within but from without and that would seem to have little or no moral content. Such religious conduct is imitative or reflex. It stems from the current cult of commotion and possesses no sound inner life.

The message "Christ in you, the hope of glory" (Colossians 1:27) needs to be restored to the Church. We must show a new generation of nervous, almost frantic, Christians that power lies at the center of the life. Speed and noise are evidences of weakness, not strength. Eternity is silent; time is noisy. Our preoccupation with time is sad evidence of our basic want of faith. The desire to be dramatically active is proof of our religious infantilism; it is a type of exhibitionism common to the kindergarten.

Questions for Reflection
To Be or to Do

1. The symmetry of character reflected in the balance between *being* and *doing* is extremely difficult to achieve. The doing should flow out of the being. However, as Tozer has observed, "In our modern civilized society the stress falls almost wholly upon doing." What is the impact of this imbalance on our daily walk of faith?

2. "Modern Christians lack symmetry," Tozer says. "They know almost nothing about the inner life. They are like a temple that is all exterior without any interior." If we lack this divine symmetry, how do we return to the proper biblical balance? Why is correcting this imbalance so urgent for individual believers and for the local church?

3. Tozer says the apparent emphasis in the church today is on commotion, not devotion; externalism, not internal matters of the heart; and on noisy religious machinery, not quiet progress in the power of the Spirit. Reflect on how this statement applies to your personal spiritual life and the life of your local church. If it is true, what must be done differently?

4. Read 1 Kings 19:11–12 and meditate on the meaning of "a sound of a gentle blowing" ("still small voice," KJV). If we can only hear God speak through tornadoes, earthquakes and fire, what does that say about our faith in God and our walk?

5. "Speed and noise are evidences of weakness, not strength. Eternity is silent; time is noisy. Our preoccupation with time is sad evidence of our basic want of faith." Reflect on the past six months: Have they been characterized by a fast, hectic pace or stillness before the Lord? What has been your progress in faith in God?

This World: Playground or Battleground?

Things are for us not only what they are; they are what we hold them to be. Which is to say that our attitude toward things is likely in the long run to be more important than the things themselves.

This is a common coin of knowledge, like an old dime, worn smooth by use. Yet it bears upon it the stamp of truth and must not be rejected because it is familiar.

It is strange how a fact may remain fixed, while our interpretation of the fact changes with the generations and the years.

One such fact is the world in which we live. It is here and has been here through the centuries. It is a stable fact, quite unchanged by the passing of time, but how different is modern man's view of it from the view our fathers held. Here we see plainly how great is the power of interpretation. The world is for all of us not only what it is; it is what we believe it to be. And a tremendous load of woe or weal rides on the soundness of our interpretation.

Going no further back than the times of the founding and early development of our country, we are able to see the wide gulf between our modern attitudes and those of our fathers. In the early days, when Christianity exercised a dominant influence over American thinking, men conceived the world to be a battleground. Our fathers believed in sin and the devil and hell as constituting one force; and they believed in God and righteousness and heaven as the other. These were opposed to each other in the nature of them forever in deep, grave, irreconcilable hostility. Man, so our fathers held, had to choose sides; he could not be neutral. For him it must be life or death, heaven or hell, and if he chose to come out on God's side, he could expect open war with God's enemies. The fight would be real and deadly and would last as long as life continued here below. Men looked forward to heaven as a return from the wars, a laying down of the sword to enjoy in peace the home prepared for them.

Sermons and songs in those days often had a martial quality about them, or perhaps a trace of homesickness. The Christian soldier thought of home and rest and reunion, and his voice grew plaintive as he sang of battle ended and victory won. But whether he was charging into enemy guns or dreaming of war's end and the Father's welcome home, he never forgot what kind of world he lived in. It was a battleground, and many were the wounded and the slain.

That view of things is unquestionably the scriptural one. Allowing for the figures and metaphors with which the Scriptures abound, it still is a solid Bible doctrine that tremendous spiritual forces are present in the world, and man, because of his spiritual nature, is caught in the middle. The evil powers are bent upon destroying him, while Christ is present to save him through the power of the gospel. To obtain deliverance, he must come out on God's side in faith and obedience. That in brief is what our fathers thought; and that, we believe, is what the Bible teaches.

How different today. The fact remains the same, but the interpretation has changed completely. Men think of the world not as a battleground but as a playground. We are not here to fight; we are here to frolic. We are not in a foreign land; we are at home. We are not getting ready to live; we are already living, and the best we can do is to rid ourselves of our inhibitions and our frustrations and live this life to the full. This, we believe, is a fair summary of the religious philosophy of modern man, openly professed by millions and tacitly held by more multiplied millions who live out that philosophy without having given verbal expression to it.

This changed attitude toward the world has had and is having its effect upon Christians, even gospel Christians who profess the faith of the Bible. By a curious juggling of the figures, they manage to add up the column wrong and yet claim to have the right answer. It sounds fantastic but it is true.

That this world is a playground instead of a battleground has now been accepted in practice by the vast majority of evangelical Christians. They might hedge around the question if they were asked bluntly to declare their position, but their conduct gives them away. They are facing both ways, enjoying Christ and the world too, and gleefully telling everyone that accepting Jesus does not require them to give up their fun and that Christianity is just the jolliest thing imaginable.

The "worship" growing out of such a view of life is as far off center as the view itself, a sort of sanctified nightclubbing without the champagne and the dressed-up drunks.

This whole thing has grown to be so serious of late that it now becomes the bounden duty of every Christian to reexamine his spiritual philosophy in the light of the Bible, and having discovered the scriptural way to follow it, even if to do so he must separate himself from much that he formerly accepted as real but which now in the light of truth he knows to be false.

A right view of God and the world to come requires that we have also a right view of the world

in which we live and our relation to it. So much de-
pends upon this that we cannot afford to be careless
about it.

Questions for Reflection
This World: Playground or Battleground?

1. "In the early days, when Christianity exercised a dominant influence over American thinking, men conceived the world to be a battleground. Our fathers believed in sin and the devil and hell as constituting one force; and they believed in God and righteousness and heaven as the other." Life was a spiritual war, so our fathers held, and we could not be neutral; we had to choose sides. "The fight would be real and deadly and would last as long as life continued here below." If, as Tozer says, this viewpoint is more in accord with Scripture than contemporary religious attitudes, what are the dangers in ignoring this spiritual battle? What role does prayer play in developing the habit of seeing the world as a battleground?

2. If the world is truly a battleground littered with the wounded and slain, then by faith what should my perspective of ministry be every day? Meditate on Ephesians 6:10–17 with this perspective in mind.

3. If I view this world as a playground instead of a battleground, then my priorities of life, not my words, will reveal it. List the top five priorities of your life. Are these priorities in line with God's priorities (Matthew 6:33)? If not, how do your priorities need to change in light of a battleground perspective?

4. Tozer notes that most Christians would not like to admit that they see the world as a playground, "but their conduct gives them away. They are facing both ways, enjoying Christ and the world too." Why is this mind-set so destructive to our faith, our evangelism and our discipleship of others in Christ?

5. Think through what Tozer means in this statement about believers with a playground mentality: "The 'worship' growing out of such a view of life is as far off center as the view itself, a sort of sanctified nightclubbing without the champagne and the dressed-up drunks."

HARD ISSUES OF FAITH

Chapter 25

Not All Faith Pleases God

W ithout faith it is impossible to please [God]," (Hebrews 11:6) but not all faith pleases God.

I do not recall another period when faith was as popular as it is today. After the First World War, the man of faith was considered weak and frightfully behind the intellectual parade. But since the close of World War II, the pendulum has swung far in the other direction. Faith has come back into favor with almost everybody. The scientist, the cab driver, the philosopher, the actress, the politician, the prize fighter, the housewife—all are ready to recommend faith as the panacea for all our ills, moral, spiritual and economic.

If we only believe hard enough, we'll make it somehow. So goes the popular chant. What you believe is not important. Only believe. Jew, Catholic, nature mystic, deist, occultist, swami, Mormon, Sufi, moonstruck poet without religious convictions, political dreamer or aspirant for a cottage on Uranus or Mars—just keep on believing, and peace, it will be wonderful. Soon a disease-free, warless world will emerge from the mists inhabited by a colorless, creedless, classless race where men will brothers be for a' that and a' that.

Back of this is the nebulous idea that faith is an almighty power flowing through the universe, which anyone may plug into at will. It is conceived vaguely as a subrational creative pulsation streaming down from somewhere Up There, ready at any time to enter our hearts and change our whole mental and moral constitution as well as our total outlook on man, God and the cosmos. When it comes in, out go pessimism, fear, defeat and failure; in come optimism, confidence, personal mastery and unfailing success in war, love, sports, business and politics.

All of this is, of course, a gossamer of self-deception woven of the unsubstantial threads of fancy spun out of minds of tenderhearted persons who want to believe it. It is a kind of poor man's transcendentalism that, in the form we have with us today, came down from the more literary and respectable transcendentalism of the New England of a century ago.

Transcendentalism is a sort of creedless religion,

growing out of the will to believe and an unwillingness to believe the Holy Scriptures. To discover the
tenets of transcendentalism is extremely difficult,
if indeed any such tenets actually exist; but Emerson gave us a hint when he said, "Belief consists in
accepting the affirmations of the soul; unbelief, in
denying them." I think this may be taken as a fair
summary of Emerson's religious belief, and certainly it is an accurate description of the humanistic
faith of the quasi-Christian masses today.

What is overlooked in all this is that faith is good
only when it engages truth; when it is made to rest
upon falsehood, it can and often does lead to eternal tragedy. For it is not enough that we believe; we
must believe the right thing about the right One. To
believe in God is more than to believe that He exists. Ahab and Judas believed that. To a right faith,
knowledge is necessary. We must know at least
something of what God is like and what His will
is for His human creatures. To know less than this
is to be thrown back upon the necessity of accepting the affirmations of the soul and substituting
"Thus saith my soul" for the biblical "Thus saith
the Lord."

True faith requires that we believe everything
God has said about Himself, but also that we believe everything He has said about us. Until we
believe that we are as bad as God says we are, we
can never believe that He will do for us what He
says He will do. Right here is where popular reli-

gion breaks down. It never quite accepts the severity of God or the depravity of man. It stresses the goodness of God and man's misfortune. Sin is a pardonable frailty, and God is not too much concerned about it. He merely wants us to trust in His goodness.

To believe thus is to ground faith upon falsehood and build our eternal hope upon sand. No man has any right to pick and choose among revealed truths. God has spoken. We are all under solemn obligation to hear the affirmations of the Holy Spirit.

To manipulate the Scriptures so as to make them excuse us, compliment us and console us is to do despite to the written Word and to reject the living Word. To believe savingly in Jesus Christ is to believe all He has said about Himself and all that the prophets and apostles have said about Him. Let us beware that the Jesus we "accept" is not one we have created out of the dust of our imagination and formed after our own likeness.

True faith commits us to obedience. "We have received grace and apostleship," says Paul, "for obedience to the faith among all nations, for his name" (Romans 1:5). That dreamy, sentimental faith that ignores the judgments of God against us and listens to the affirmations of the soul is as deadly as cyanide. That faith that passively accepts all the pleasant texts of the Scriptures while it overlooks or rejects the stern warnings and commandments of those same Scriptures is not the faith of which

Christ and His apostles spoke.

Faith in faith is faith astray. To hope for heaven by means of such faith is to drive in the dark across a deep chasm on a bridge that doesn't quite reach the other side.

Questions for Reflection
Not All Faith Pleases God

1. "Belief consists in accepting the affirmations of the soul; unbelief, in denying them" are the words of Emerson. Tozer notes that this summary of Emerson's religious belief is certainly "an accurate description of the humanistic faith of the quasi-Christian masses today." Reflect on Emerson's perspective of belief and Tozer's assessment of it today. If Tozer's assessment is true, how does that explain the difficulties in evangelism and in presenting believers complete in Christ today?

2. "For it is not enough that we believe; we must believe the right thing about the right One." Where do we learn the right things about the right One, and how must that learning be enabled? Make a list of things you could do to fortify your understanding and belief in the Righteous and Holy One.

3. True faith not only believes everything that God says about Himself, but also everything He says about us. "Until we believe that we are as bad as God says we are, we can never believe that He will do for us what He says He will do." Why is acceptance of man's total depravity critical to our understanding of God and our walk in faith?

4. "True faith commits us to obedience." This is not a partial obedience where we pick and choose from the Bible what to believe and follow. If we choose pleasant or encouraging Scripture passages that lift us up, we cannot ignore stern warnings and commandments that make us uncomfortable. True faith commits us to complete obedience. Think of a time in your life that was characterized by partial obedience and weak faith, as well as a time that was characterized by a stronger obedience. Contrast the two time periods in the areas of faith in God and service to others.

5. "Faith in faith is faith astray." Discuss the destructive aspects of this kind of faith. How does one change the focus of faith on God and His Word and not just on faith?

Chapter 26

Faith Dares to Fail

In this world men are judged by their ability to do. They are rated according to the distance they have come up the hill of achievement. At the bottom is utter failure at the top complete success; and between these two extremes the majority of civilized men sweat and struggle from youth to old age.

A few give up, slide to the bottom and become inhabitants of skid row. There, with ambition gone and will broken, they subsist on handouts till nature forecloses on them and death takes them away. At the top are the few who by a combination of talent, hard work and good fortune manage to reach the peak and all the luxury, fame and power that are found there.

But in all of this there is no happiness. The effort to succeed puts too much strain on the nerves. Excessive preoccupation with the struggle to win narrows the mind, hardens the heart and shuts out a thousand bright visions that might be enjoyed if there were only leisure to notice them.

The man who reaches the pinnacle is seldom happy for very long. He soon becomes eaten by fears that he may slip back a peg and be forced to surrender his place to another. Examples of this are found in the feverish way the TV star watches his rating and the politician his mail.

Let an elected official learn that a poll shows him to be 2 percent less popular in August than he was in March and he begins to sweat like a man on his way to prison. The ballplayer lives by his averages, the businessman by his rising graph and the concert star by his applause meter. It is not uncommon for a challenger in the ring to weep openly when he fails to knock out the champion. To be second best leaves him completely disconsolate; he must be first to be happy.

This mania to succeed is a good thing perverted. The desire to fulfill the purpose for which we were created is of course a gift from God, but sin has twisted this impulse about and turned it into a selfish lust for first place and top honors. By this lust the whole world of mankind is driven as by a demon, and there is no escape.

When we come to Christ, we enter a different world. The New Testament introduces us to a spiri-

tual philosophy infinitely higher than and altogether contrary to that which motivates the world. According to the teaching of Christ, the poor in spirit
are blessed; the meek inherit the earth; the first are
last and the last first; the greatest man is the one
who best serves others; the one who loses everything is the only one who will have everything at
last; the successful man of the world will see his
hoarded treasures swept away by the tempest of
judgment; the righteous beggar goes to Abraham's
bosom and the rich man burns in the fires of hell.

Our Lord died an apparent failure, discredited
by the leaders of established religion, rejected by
society and forsaken by His friends. The man who
ordered Him to the cross was the successful states-
man whose hand the ambitious hack politician
kissed. It took the resurrection to demonstrate how
gloriously Christ had triumphed and how tragical-
ly the governor had failed.

Yet today the professed church seems to have
learned nothing. We are still seeing as men see and
judging after the manner of man's judgment. How
much eager-beaver religious work is done out of a
carnal desire to make good. How many hours of
prayer are wasted beseeching God to bless projects
that are geared to the glorification of little men. How
much sacred money is poured out upon men who,
in spite of their tear-in-the-voice appeals, nevertheless seek only to make a fair show in the flesh.

The true Christian should turn away from all this.

Especially should ministers of the gospel search their own hearts and look deep into their inner motives. No man is worthy to succeed until he is willing to fail. No man is morally worthy of success in religious activities until he is willing that the honor of succeeding should go to another if God so wills.

God may allow His servant to succeed when He has disciplined him to a point where he does not need to succeed to be happy. The man who is elated by success and cast down by failure is still a carnal man. At best his fruit will have a worm in it.

God will allow His servant to succeed when he has learned that success does not make him dearer to God nor more valuable in the total scheme of things. We cannot buy God's favor with crowds or converts or new missionaries sent out or Bibles distributed. All these things can be accomplished without the help of the Holy Spirit. A good personality and a shrewd knowledge of human nature are all that any man needs to be a success in religious circles today.

Our great honor lies in being just what Jesus was and is. To be accepted by those who accept Him, rejected by all who reject Him, loved by those who love Him and hated by everyone who hates Him. What greater glory could come to any man?

We can afford to follow Him to failure. Faith dares to fail. The resurrection and the judgment will demonstrate before all worlds who won and who lost. We can wait.

Questions for Reflection
Faith Dares to Fail

1. In this day and age, men are judged by their suc-
    cess, but there is little happiness at reaching the pin-
    nacle. Instead, "the effort to succeed puts too much
    strain on the nerves. Excessive preoccupation with
    the struggle to win narrows the mind, hardens the
    heart," and robs the individual of the time to enjoy
    the honest fruits of his labor. Reflect upon the con-
    suming nature of the drive for success and how it
    can undermine our faith in God.

2. Tozer notes that we all have an impulse to fulfill the
    purpose for which we were created, but "sin has
    twisted this impulse about and turned it into a self-
    ish lust for first place and top honors. By this lust the
    whole world of mankind is driven as by a demon,
    and there is no escape." What are the manifestations
    of this drive to succeed? How does one leave one's
    success or failure in the hands of God? What lessons
    can we learn in this area from the life of Christ?

3. "Yet today the professed church seems to have
    learned nothing. We are still seeing as men see and
    judging after the manner of man's judgment. How
    much eager-beaver religious work is done out of a
    carnal desire to make good?" Discuss or reflect on
    this statement by Tozer.

4. Have you personally experienced failure? Make a list of your two biggest failures. Can you agree with Tozer that "no man is worthy to succeed until he is willing to fail" and that "no man is morally worthy of success in religious activities until he is willing that the honor of succeeding should go to another if God so wills"? How did your failures cause your faith to grow stronger?

5. Moses' striking of the rock at Meribah (see Numbers 20:1–13) shows that if we don't follow the Lord's way, we may have outward success in the religious or personal world, but sooner or later we will pay a penalty. In that light, how does one evaluate successes and failures before the Lord? "God will allow His servant to succeed when he has learned that success does not make him dearer to God nor more valuable in the total scheme of things." How does the statement by Tozer lead us into freedom in Christ?

6. "We can afford to follow Him to failure. Faith dares to fail. The resurrection and the judgment will demonstrate before all worlds who won and who lost. We can wait." The Scriptures say that "none of those who wait for You will be ashamed" (Psalm 25:3). Reflect on how our impatience for results affects our faith in God. How should a believer deal with such attitudes as impatience for results and an unwillingness to fail?

Chapter 27

The Sacrament of Living

*Whether therefore ye eat, or drink, or whatsoever ye do,
do all to the glory of God. (1 Corinthians 10:31)*

One of the greatest hindrances to internal peace that the Christian encounters is the common habit of dividing our lives into two areas: the sacred and the secular. As these areas are conceived to exist apart from each other and to be morally and spiritually incompatible, and as we are compelled by the necessities of living to be always crossing back and forth from the one to the other, our inner lives tend to break up so that we live a divided instead of a unified life.

Our trouble springs from the fact that we who follow Christ inhabit at once two worlds—the spiritual and the natural. As children of Adam, we live our lives on earth subject to the limitations of the flesh and the weaknesses and ills to which human nature is heir. Merely to live among men requires of us years of hard toil and much care and attention to the things of this world. In sharp contrast to this is our life in the Spirit. There we enjoy another and higher kind of life—we are children of God; we possess heavenly status and enjoy intimate fellowship with Christ.

This tends to divide our total life into two departments. We come unconsciously to recognize two sets of actions. The first are performed with a feeling of satisfaction and a firm assurance that they are pleasing to God. These are the sacred acts and they are usually thought to be prayer, Bible reading, hymn singing, church attendance and such other acts as spring directly from faith. They may be known by the fact that they have no direct relation to this world, and would have no meaning whatever except as faith shows us another world, "an house not made with hands, eternal in the heavens" (2 Corinthians 5:1).

Over against these sacred acts are the secular ones. They include all of the ordinary activities of life that we share with the sons and daughters of Adam: eating, sleeping, working, looking after the needs of the body and performing our dull and prosaic duties here on earth. These we often do reluctantly and with many misgivings, often apologizing to God for what we consider a waste of time and strength. The upshot of this is that we are uneasy most of the time. We go about our common tasks with a feeling of deep frustration, telling ourselves pensively that there's a better day coming when we shall slough off this earthly shell and be bothered no more with the affairs of this world.

This is the old sacred-secular antithesis. Most Christians are caught in its trap. They cannot get a satisfactory adjustment between the claims of the two worlds. They try to walk the tightrope between two kingdoms, and they find no peace in either. Their strength is reduced, their outlook confused and their joy taken from them.

I believe this state of affairs to be wholly unnecessary. We have gotten ourselves on the horns of a dilemma, true enough, but the dilemma is not real. It is a creature of misunderstanding. The sacred-secular antithesis has no foundation in the New Testament. Without doubt, a more perfect understanding of Christian truth will deliver us from it.

The Lord Jesus Christ Himself is our perfect example, and He knew no divided life. In the presence of His Father, He lived on earth without strain from babyhood to His death on the cross. God accepted the offering of His total life, and made no distinction between act and act. "I do always those things that please him," was His brief summary of His own life as it related to the Father (John 8:29). As He moved among men, He was poised and restful. What pressure and suffering He endured grew out of His position as the world's sin bearer; they were never the result of moral uncertainty or spiritual maladjustment.

Paul's exhortation to "do all to the glory of God" (1 Corinthians 10:31) is more than pious idealism. It is an integral part of the sacred revelation and is to be accepted as the very Word of Truth. It opens before us the possibility of making every act of our lives contribute to the glory of God. Lest we should be too timid to include everything, Paul mentions specifically eating and drinking. This humble privilege we share with the beasts that perish. If these lowly animal acts can be so performed as to honor God, then it becomes difficult to conceive of one that cannot.

That monkish hatred of the body that figures so prominently in the works of certain early devotional writers is wholly without support in the Word of God. Common modesty is found in the sacred Scriptures, it is true, but never prudery or a false sense of shame. The New Testament accepts as a matter of course that in His incarnation our Lord took upon Him a real human body, and no effort is made to steer around the downright implications of such a fact. He lived in that body here among men and never once performed a nonsacred act. His presence in human flesh sweeps away forever the evil notion that there is about the human body something innately offensive to the Deity. God created our bodies, and we do not offend Him by placing the responsibility where it belongs. He is not ashamed of the work of His own hands.

Perversion, misuse and abuse of our human powers should give us cause enough to be ashamed. Bodily acts done in sin and contrary to nature can never honor God. Wherever the human will introduces moral evil, we have no longer our innocent and harmless powers as God made them; we have instead an abused and twisted thing that can never bring glory to its Creator.

Let us, however, assume that perversion and abuse are not present. Let us think of a Christian believer in whose life the twin wonders of repentance and the new birth have been wrought. He is now living according to the will of God as he understands it from the written Word. Of such a one it may be said that every act of his life is or can be as truly sacred as prayer or baptism or the Lord's Supper. To say this is not to bring all acts down to one dead level; it is rather to lift every act up into a living kingdom and turn the whole life into a sacrament.

If a sacrament is an external expression of an inward grace, then we need not hesitate to accept the above thesis. By one act of consecration of our total selves to God, we can make every subsequent act express that consecration. We need no more be ashamed of our body—the fleshly servant that carries us through life—than Jesus was of the humble beast upon which He rode into Jerusalem. "The Lord hath need of [him]" (Matthew 21:3) may well apply to our mortal bodies. If Christ dwells in us, we may bear about the Lord of glory as the little beast did of old and give occasion to the multitudes to cry, "Hosanna in the highest!"

That we see this truth is not enough. If we would escape from the toils of the sacred-secular dilemma, the truth must "run in our blood" and condition the complex of our thoughts. We must practice living to the glory of God, actually and determinedly. By meditation upon this truth, by talking it over with God often in our prayers, by recalling it to our minds frequently as we move about among men, a sense of its wondrous meaning will take hold of us. The old painful duality will go down before a restful unity of life. The knowledge that we are all God's, that He has received all and rejected nothing, will unify our inner lives and make everything sacred to us.

This is not quite all. Long-held habits do not die easily. It will take intelligent thought and a great deal of reverent prayer to escape completely from the sacred-secular psychology. For instance, it may be difficult for the average Christian to get hold of the idea that his daily labors can be performed as acts of worship acceptable to God by Jesus Christ. The old antithesis will crop up in the back of his head sometimes to disturb his peace of mind. Nor will that old serpent, the devil, take all this lying down. He will be there in the cab or at the desk or in the field to remind the Christian that he is giving the better part of his day to the things of this world and allotting to his religious duties only a trifling portion of his time. And unless great care is taken, this will create confusion and bring discouragement and heaviness of heart.

We can meet this successfully only by the exercise of an aggressive faith. We must offer all our acts to God and believe that He accepts them. Then hold firmly to that position and keep insisting that every act of every hour of the day and night be included in the transaction. Keep reminding God in our times of private prayer that we mean every act for His glory; then supplement those times by a thousand thought-prayers as we go about the job of living. Let us practice the fine art of making every work a priestly ministration. Let us believe that God is in all our simple deeds and learn to find Him there.

A concomitant of the error that we have been discussing is the sacred-secular antithesis as applied to places. It is little short of astonishing that we can read the New Testament and still believe in the inherent sacredness of some places. This error is so widespread that one feels all alone when he tries to combat it. It has acted as a kind of dye to color the thinking of religious persons and has colored the eyes as well so that it is all but impossible to detect its fallacy. In the face of every New Testament teaching to the contrary, it has been said and sung throughout the centuries and accepted as a part of the Christian message, that which it most surely is not. Only the Quakers, so far as my knowledge goes, have had the perception to see the error and the courage to expose it.

Here are the facts as I see them. For four hundred years Israel had dwelt in Egypt, surrounded by the crassest idolatry. By the hand of Moses, they were brought out at last and started toward the land of promise. The very idea of holiness had been lost to them. To correct this, God began at the bottom. He localized Himself in the cloud and fire, and later when the tabernacle had been built, He dwelt in fiery manifestation in the Holy of Holies. By innumerable distinctions God taught Israel the difference between holy and unholy. There were holy days, holy vessels, holy garments. There were washings, sacrifices, offerings of many kinds. By these means, Israel learned that God is holy. It was this that He was teaching them, not the holiness of things or places. The holiness of Jehovah was the lesson they must learn.

Then came the great day when Christ appeared. Immediately He began to say, "Ye have heard that it was said by them of old time . . . but I say unto you" (Matthew 5:21–22). The Old Testament schooling was over. When Christ died on the cross, the veil of the temple was rent from top to bottom. The Holy of Holies was opened to everyone who would enter in faith. Christ's words were remembered:

> The hour cometh, when ye shall neither in this
> mountain, nor yet at Jerusalem, worship the
> Father. . . . But the hour cometh, and now is, when
> the true worshippers shall worship the Father in
> spirit and in truth: for the Father seeketh such to
> worship him. God is a Spirit: and they that worship
> him must worship him in spirit and in truth.
> (John 4:21, 23–24)

Shortly after, Paul took up the cry of liberty and declared all meats clean, every day holy, all places sacred and every act acceptable to God. The sacredness of times and places, a half-light necessary to the education of the race, passed away before the full sun of spiritual worship.

The essential spirituality of worship remained the possession of the church until it was slowly lost with the passing of the years. Then the natural *legality* of the fallen hearts of men began to introduce the old distinctions. The church came to observe again days and seasons and times. Certain places were chosen and marked out as holy in a special sense. Differences were observed between one and another day or place or person. The "sacraments" were first two, then three, then four, until with the triumph of Romanism, they were fixed at seven.

In all charity, and with no desire to reflect unkindly upon any Christian, however misled, I would point out that the Roman Catholic Church represents today the sacred-secular heresy carried to its logical conclusion. Its deadliest effect is the complete cleavage it introduces between religion and life. Its teachers attempt to avoid this snare by many footnotes and multitudinous explanations, but the mind's instinct for logic is too strong. In practical living the cleavage is a fact.

From this bondage reformers and puritans and mystics have labored to free us. Today, the trend in conservative circles is back toward that bondage again. It is said that a horse, after it has been led out of a burning building, will sometimes, by a strange obstinacy, break loose from its rescuer and dash back into the building again to perish in the flame. By some such stubborn tendency toward error, fundamentalism in our day is moving back toward spiritual slavery. The observation of days and times is becoming more and more prominent among us. "Lent" and "holy week" and "good" Friday are words heard more and more frequently upon the lips of gospel Christians. We do not know when we are well off.

In order that I may be understood and not be misunderstood, I would throw into relief the practical implications of the teaching for which I have been arguing (i.e., the sacramental quality of everyday living). Against its positive meanings, I should like to point out a few things it does not mean.

It does not mean, for instance, that everything we do is of equal importance with everything else we do or may do. One act of a good man's life may differ widely from another in importance. Paul's sewing of tents was not equal to his writing of an edpistle to the Romans, but both were accepted of God and both were true acts of worship. Certainly it is more important to lead a soul to Christ than to plant a garden, but the planting of the garden *can* be as holy an act as the winning of a soul.

Again, it does not mean that every man is as useful as every other man. Gifts differ in the body of Christ. A Billy Bray is not to be compared with a Luther or a Wesley for sheer usefulness to the church and to the world; but the service of the less gifted brother is as pure as that of the more gifted, and God accepts both with equal pleasure.

The "layman" need never think of his humbler task as being inferior to that of his minister. "Let every man abide in the same calling wherein he was called" (1 Corinthinas 7:20), and his work will be as sacred as the work of the ministry. It is not what a man does that determines whether his work is sacred or secular, it is why he does it. The motive is everything. Let a man sanctify the Lord God in his heart and he can thereafter do no common act. All he does is good and acceptable to God through Jesus Christ. For such a man, living itself will be a priestly ministration. As he performs his never-so-simple task, he will hear the voice of the seraphim saying, "Holy, holy, holy, is the LORD of hosts: the whole earth is full of his glory" (Isaiah 6:3).

Lord, I would trust Thee completely; I would be alto-gether Thine; I would exalt Thee above all. I desire that I may feel no sense of possessing anything outside of Thee. I want constantly to be aware of Thy overshadowing presence and to hear Thy speaking voice. I long to live in restful sincerity of heart. I want to live so fully in the Spirit that all my thoughts may be as sweet incense ascending to Thee and every act of my life may be an act of worship. Therefore I pray in the words of Thy great servant of old, "I beseech Thee so for to cleanse the intent of mine heart with the unspeakable gift of Thy grace, that I may perfectly love Thee and worthily praise Thee." And all this I confidently believe Thou wilt grant me through the merits of Jesus Christ Thy Son. Amen.

Questions for Reflection
The Sacrament of Living

1. Tozer observes that one of the greatest hindrances to internal peace and progress in faith is "the common habit of dividing our lives into two areas—the sacred and the secular." However, the Lord Jesus Christ Himself knew no divided life "for I always do the things that are pleasing to Him" (John 8:29). Thus, walking by faith makes all of life sacred as we follow the One who "never once performed a non-sacred act." How do we cultivate this mind-set and lifestyle? Reflect on your "secular" activities for the past week. What steps of faith were taken?

2. "If we would escape from the toils of the sacred-secular dilemma, the truth must 'run in our blood' and condition the complex of our thoughts. We must practice living to the glory of God, actually and determinedly." In fact, Tozer notes success in this struggle is only possible by the exercise of "aggressive faith." What does he mean by aggressive faith? How can a mentoring or discipleship relationship help a believer in this area?

3. Do you see God's hand in the "secular" activities and duties that you are involved in at work, home or leisure? If we do not, how can we see God's hand

in the "sacred"? Why must this sacred-secular dilemma be resolved for our faith "to excel still more" (1 Thessalonians 4:1, 10)?

4. "It is not what a man does that determines whether his work is sacred or secular; it is why he does it. The motive is everything." If the believer has sought to glorify God in all he does by faith ("for apart from Me you can do nothing" John 15:5), then living itself will be a priestly ministry on hallowed ground. It takes faith to see this hallowed ground, and it takes faith to act righteously on this hallowed ground. How do we recognize this hallowed ground? How do we judge our motives? How do we return to a walk of faith when we realize our motives are incorrect?

Chapter 28

Understanding Those
Dry Spells

Probably nothing else bothers the earnest Christian quite so much as the problem of those dry spells that come to him occasionally, no matter how faithfully he tries to obey God and walk in the light. He can never predict them, and he cannot explain them. And there lies the difficulty.

It might comfort one who finds himself in the middle of an emotional desert to know that his experience is not unique. The sweetest and holiest saints whose feet have graced this earth have at some time found themselves there. The books of devotion that have come to us from the past almost all have at least one chapter dealing with what some of them call "aridity" in the Christian life. The very word itself tempts us to smile in sympathy, for it so perfectly describes the experience so many of us know only too well. Our heart feels "arid" and nothing we can do will bring the rain. It is good to know during such an internal drought that it has been a common experience with the saints.

One reason for our distress at such times is the knowledge that sin is one cause of aridity in the life; we naturally reason that if sin brings drought and we are suffering a dry spell, then we must have been guilty of sin whether we knew it or not. The way to deal with the problem is to remember that *sin is not the only cause of dryness.* If after an honest examination of our lives, we are sure that we are not living in a state of disobedience and that no past sin is unforgiven, we may dismiss sin as the cause of our dry condition. We do God no honor and ourselves no good by assuming that we have sinned if we have not. Indeed we play straight into Satan's hands by accepting the morbid suggestion that somewhere in the mysterious depths of our nature there must be some sin that is displeasing God and causing Him to hide His face from us. What God has cleansed we should not call unclean; to do so would be unbelief.

"Religion," say the theologians, "lies in the will." What our will is set to do is what really matters at last. Aridity has nothing to do with the will. "If any man will," said Jesus; He did not say, "If any man feel." Feeling is the play of emotion over the will, a kind of musical accompaniment to the business of living, and while it is indeed most enjoyable to have the band play as we march to Zion, it is by no means indispensable. We can work and walk without music, and if we have true faith we can walk with God without feeling.

Normally we may expect some degree of spiritual joy to be present most of the time. Fellowship with God is so delightful that it cannot but provide a large measure of joy; but we are talking now about those times when our joy fades out and the presence of the Lord is felt feebly or not at all. Such times demand that we exercise faith. Moments of great spiritual delight do not require much faith; if we never come down from the mount of blessing, we might easily come to trust in our own delights rather than in the unshakable character of God. It is necessary therefore that our watchful heavenly Father withdraw His inward comforts from us sometimes to teach us that Christ alone is the Rock upon which we must repose our everlasting trust.

Questions for Reflection
Understanding Those Dry Spells

1.   There is no doubt that the Christian who truly wants to please God will occasionally experience dry spells where the "heart feels arid and nothing we can do will bring the rain." Tozer rightly notes that these times cannot be predicted or explained, but in the sovereignty of God these internal droughts have been allowed for the earnest believer and have been common to saints throughout history. Have you ever learned something new about God while in a dry spell? How was your faith affected? If you have never experienced a dry spell, think about how you might prepare for such an unpredictable event.

2.   Tozer makes it very clear that "sin is not the only cause of dryness." To say that sin is the cause when it is not does not honor God and creates serious tensions in the believer's heart. To say that the cause is something else when it is sin is wrong as well because our relationship with the Father is affected. What steps can we take to determine the cause of a dry spell? If we cannot determine the cause, what must we continue to do?

3.   "Aridity has nothing to do with the will. 'If any man will,' said Jesus; He did not say, 'If any man feel.'" If we truly understand walking by faith in God, we

can do so without feeling. If you have experienced a dry spell, what were your feelings like during that time? What encouraged you the most in that time?

4. These dry spells are times "when our joy fades out and the presence of the Lord is felt only feebly or not at all." These times may be short or long in duration, but surely such times will require us to exercise faith. Looking back on any dry spell experiences you may have experienced, describe the process you went through. In light of Isaiah 50:10 and Job 23:8–17, as well as Tozer's comments, what would you do differently now?

5. "Moments of great spiritual delight do not require much faith; if we never come down from the mount of blessing, we might easily come to trust in our own delights rather than the unshakable character of God." In light of this truth, we can see that even dry spells or internal droughts are ministers of God (Psalm 119:91). Meditate on or discuss these truths, especially as they relate to our faith in Christ growing still more.

Chapter 29

On to El-beth-el!

Jacob, after his memorable experience in the wilderness, where he saw a ladder set up on the earth and saw God standing above it, called the place of his encounter Beth-el, which means "the house of God," *beth* being house and *el*, God.

Many years later, after he had suffered and sinned and repented and discovered the worthlessness of all earthly things, had been conquered and blessed by God at Peniel and had seen the face of God in an hour of spiritual agony, he renamed the place *El-beth-el*, which means "the God of the house of God." Historically the place was always known as Bethel, but in Jacob's worshipping heart it would forever be El Bethel.

The change is significant. Jacob had shifted his

emphasis from the house to the One whom he met there. God Himself now took the center of his interest. He had at last been converted from a place to God Himself. A blessed conversion.

Many Christians never get beyond Beth-el. God is in their thoughts, but He is not first. His name is spoken only after a hyphen has separated the primary interest from the secondary, God being secondary, the "house" first. The weakness of the denominational psychology is that it puts something else before God. Certainly there may be no intention to do so; the very thought may startle the innocent denominationalist; but where the emphasis is, there the heart is also. Loyalty to our group may be a fine thing, but when it puts God on the other side of a hyphen, it is a bad thing. Always God must be first.

Faithfulness to the local church is also a good thing. The true Christian will, by a kind of spiritual instinct, find a body of believers somewhere, identify himself with it and try by every proper means to promote its growth and prosperity. And that, we repeat, is good. But when the church becomes so large and important that it hides God from our eyes, it is no longer for us a good thing. Or better say that it is a good thing wrongly used. For the church was never intended to substitute for God. Let us understand that every local church embraces El-beth-el and the right balance will be found and maintained: God first and His house second.

I sometimes fear that theology itself may exist as a semiopaque veil behind which God, if seen at all, is seen only imperfectly. Theology is precious because it is the study of God. And the very English word in its composition puts God where He belongs—first. But God is often anything but first in much that is called theology. Too frequently He "standeth behind our wall, he looketh forth at the windows, shewing himself through the lattice" (Song of Solomon 2:9). We talk endlessly about Him and fail completely to notice Him as He tries to attract our attention in actual experience.

Every means of grace is but a "house," a "place," and God must be there to make it significant. Any means that can be disassociated from God can be a snare if we do not watch it. It has not done anything for us till it has led us to God and put an *El* after it. But still it is incomplete, and will be until the *El* is placed before it. No soul has found its real place till all its places have God before them: God first—God on the near side of the hyphen. We may judge our spiritual growth pretty accurately by observing the total emphasis of our heart. Where is the primary interest? Is it Beth-el or El-beth-el? Is it my church or my Lord? Is it my ministry or my God? My creed or my Christ? We are spiritual or carnal just as we are concerned with the house or with the God of the house. If we discover that religious things are first, separated from God by a hyphen, we should immediately go down in tender penitence before our

Lord and pray that He will forgive us for this affront and correct our evil attitude. He will hear and, if we continue to seek Him in sincerity of heart, He will take His place in the center of our lives where He by every right belongs.

When we have gone on from Beth-el to El-bethel, the Triune God will become to us our home, our environment, our rest and our life. Then we shall know the deep, inner meaning of the Christian faith; but not till then.

Questions for Reflection
On to El-beth-el!

1. Many Christians never get beyond Bethel (the house of God). "God is in their thoughts, but He is not first. His name is spoken only after a hyphen has separated the primary interest from the secondary, God being secondary, the house first." This distorted order not only destroys God's "house" but also the faith and walk of the individual believer. God must always be first! How can we be sure that God is not only first in our life but also in God's house where we worship?

2. "When the church becomes so large and important that it hides God from our eyes, it is no longer for us a good thing. Or better say that it is a good thing wrongly used. For the church was never intended to substitute for God." Do you ever feel God is hidden from your eyes in your local church due to tradition, bureaucracy, the power structure, formality, money, bad teaching or some other reason? What options do you have to change the situation?

3. "We may judge our spiritual growth pretty accurately by observing the total emphasis of our heart. Where is our primary interest? Is it Beth-el [the house of God] or El-beth-el [the God of the house of God]?" This is an assessment that believers need to

make frequently to avoid getting off of the path of faith. Spend some isolated time alone with the Lord and ask Him to search your heart in this arena. If He exposes wrong priorities, "immediately go down in tender penitence before our Lord and pray that He will forgive us for this affront and correct our evil attitude."

4. It should encourage us to know that Jacob's spiritual journey really began at Beth-el and over twenty years later came to El-beth-el, the God of the house of God. It may take time for God to transform us into the image of Christ, to change our heart and to order our priorities in such a way that God is first, not second. Has this been part of your journey of faith? What has God been using in your life to reorder your priorities? What has been your experience?

Chapter 30

The Gaze of the Soul

Looking unto Jesus the author and finisher
of our faith. (Hebrews 12:2)

L et us think of an intelligent, plain man coming
for the first time to the reading of the Scriptures.
He approaches the Bible without any previous
knowledge of what it contains. He is wholly without prejudice; he has nothing to prove and nothing
to defend.

Such a man will not have to read long until his
mind begins to observe certain truths standing out
from the page. They are the spiritual principles behind the record of God's dealings with men, and
woven into the writings of holy men as they "were
moved by the Holy Ghost" (2 Peter 1:21). As he

reads on he might want to number these truths as they become clear to him and make a brief summary under each number. These summaries will be the tenets of his biblical creed. Further reading will not affect these points except to enlarge and strengthen them. Our man is finding out what the Bible actually teaches.

High up on the list of things that the Bible teaches will be the doctrine of *faith*. The place of weighty importance that the Bible gives to faith will be too plain for him to miss. He will very likely conclude that faith is all-important in the life of the soul. "Without faith it is impossible to please [God]" (Hebrews 11:6). Faith will get me anything, take me anywhere in the kingdom of God, but without faith there can be no approach to God, no forgiveness, no deliverance, no salvation, no communion, no spiritual life at all.

By the time our friend has reached the 11th chapter of Hebrews the eloquent encomium that is there pronounced upon faith will not seem strange to him. He will have read Paul's powerful defense of faith in his Roman and Galatian epistles. Later, if he goes on to study church history, he will understand the amazing power in the teachings of the Reformers as they showed the central place of faith in the Christian religion.

Now if faith is so vitally important, if it is an indispensable must in our pursuit of God, it is perfectly natural that we should be deeply concerned over whether or not we possess this most precious gift. And our minds being what they are, it is inevitable that sooner or later we should get around to inquiring after the nature of faith. What is faith? would lie close to the question, Do I have faith? and would demand an answer if it were anywhere to be found.

Almost all who preach or write on the subject of faith have much the same things to say concerning it. They tell us that it is believing a promise, that it is taking God at His word, that it is reckoning the Bible to be true and stepping out upon it. The rest of the book or sermon is usually taken up with stories of persons who have had their prayers answered as a result of their faith. These answers are mostly direct gifts of a practical and temporal nature such as health, money, physical protection or success in business. Or if the teacher is of a philosophic turn of mind, he may take another course and lose us in a welter of metaphysics or snow us under with psychological jargon as he defines and redefines, paring the slender hair of faith thinner and thinner till it disappears in gossamer shavings at last. When he is finished, we get up disappointed and go out "by that same door where in we went." Surely there must be something better than this.

In Scripture there is practically no effort made to define faith. Outside of a brief fourteen-word definition in Hebrews 11:1, I know of no biblical definition. Even there faith is defined functionally, not philosophically; that is, it is a statement of what faith is in operation, not what it is in essence. It assumes the presence of faith and shows what it results in, rather than what it is. We will be wise to go just that far and attempt to go no further. We are told from whence it comes and by what means: "Faith . . . is the gift of God" (Ephesians 2:8) and "Faith cometh by hearing, and hearing by the word of God" (Romans 10:17). This much is clear, and, to paraphrase Thomas à Kempis, "I had rather exercise faith than know the definition thereof."

From here on, when the words *faith is* or their equivalent occur in this chapter, I ask that they be understood to refer to what faith is in operation as exercised by a believing man. Right here we drop the notion of definition and think about faith as it may be experienced in action. The complexion of our thoughts will be practical, not theoretical.

In a dramatic story in the book of Numbers (Numbers 21:4–9) faith is seen in action. Israel became discouraged and spoke against God, and the Lord sent fiery serpents among them. "And they bit the people; and much people of Israel died" (Numbers 21:6). Then Moses sought the Lord for them and He heard and gave them a remedy against the bite of the serpents. He commanded Moses to make a serpent of brass and put it upon a pole in sight of all the people, "and it shall come to pass, that every one that is bitten, when he looketh upon it, shall live" (Numbers 21:8). Moses obeyed, "and it came to pass, that if a serpent had bitten any man, when he beheld the serpent of brass, he lived" (Numbers 21:9).

In the New Testament this important bit of history is interpreted for us by no less an authority than our Lord Jesus Christ Himself. He is explaining to His hearers how they may be saved. He tells them that it is by believing. Then to make it clear, He refers to this incident in the book of Numbers. "As Moses lifted up the serpent in the wilderness, even so must the Son of man be lifted up: that whosoever believeth in him should not perish, but have eternal life" (John 3:14–15).

Our plain man, in reading this, would make an important discovery. He would notice that look and believe are synonymous terms. "Looking" on the Old Testament serpent is identical with "believing" in the New Testament Christ. That is, the looking and the believing are the same thing. And he would understand that, while Israel looked with their external eyes, believing is done with the heart. I think he would conclude *that faith is the gaze of a soul upon a saving God.*

When he had seen this, he would remember passages he had read before, and their meaning would come flooding over him. "They looked unto him, and were lightened: and their faces were not ashamed" (Psalm 34:5).

Unto thee lift I up mine eyes, O thou that dwellest in the heavens. Behold, as the eyes of servants look unto the hand of their masters, and as the eyes of a maiden unto the hand of her mistress; so our eyes wait upon the LORD our God, until that he have mercy upon us. (123:1–2)

Here the man seeking mercy looks straight at the God of mercy and never takes his eyes away from Him till He grants mercy. And our Lord Himself looked always at God. "Looking up to heaven, he blessed, and brake, and gave the loaves to his disciples" (Matthew 14:19). Indeed, Jesus taught that He wrought His works by always keeping His inward eyes upon His Father. His power lay in His continuous look at God (see John 5:19–21).

In full accord with the few texts we have quoted is the whole tenor of the inspired Word. It is summed up for us in the Hebrew epistle when we are instructed to run life's race "looking unto Jesus the author and finisher of our faith" (Hebrews 12:2). From all this we learn that faith is not a once-done act but a continuous gaze of the heart at the Triune God.

Believing, then, is directing the heart's attention to Jesus. It is lifting the mind to "Behold the Lamb of God" (John 1:29), and never ceasing that beholding for the rest of our lives. At first this may be difficult, but it becomes easier as we look steadily at His wondrous person, quietly and without strain. Distractions may hinder, but once the heart is committed to Him, after each brief excursion away from Him, the attention will return again and rest upon Him like a wandering bird coming back to its window.

I would emphasize this one committal, this one great volitional act that establishes the heart's intention to gaze forever upon Jesus. God takes this intention for our choice and makes what allowances He must for the thousand distractions that beset us in this evil world. He knows that we have set the direction of our hearts toward Jesus, and we can know it too, and comfort ourselves with the knowledge that a habit of soul is forming, which will become, after a while, a sort of spiritual reflex requiring no more conscious effort on our part.

Faith is the least self-regarding of the virtues. It is by its very nature scarcely conscious of its own existence. Like the eye that sees everything in front of it and never sees itself, faith is occupied with the Object upon which it rests and pays no attention to itself at all. While we are looking at God, we do not see ourselves—blessed riddance. The man who has struggled to purify himself and has had nothing but repeated failures will experience real relief when he stops tinkering with his soul and looks away to the perfect One. While he looks at Christ, the very things he has so long been trying to do will be getting done within him. It will be God working in him to will and to do (see Philippians 2:13).

Faith is not in itself a meritorious act; the merit is in the One toward whom it is directed. Faith is a redirecting of our sight, a getting out of the focus of our own vision and getting God into focus.

Sin has twisted our vision inward and made it self-regarding. Unbelief has put self where God should be, and is perilously close to the sin of Lucifer who said, "I will set my throne above the stars of God" (see Isaiah 14:13). Faith looks *out* instead of *in* and the whole life falls into line.

All this may seem too simple. But we have no apology to make. To those who would seek to climb into heaven after help or descend into hell, God says, "The word is nigh thee, even . . . the word of faith" (Romans 10:8). The Word induces us to lift up our eyes unto the Lord and the blessed work of faith begins.

When we lift our inward eyes to gaze upon God, we are sure to meet friendly eyes gazing back at us, for it is written that "the eyes of the LORD run to and fro throughout the whole earth" (see 2 Chronicles 16:9). The sweet language of experience is, "Thou God seest me" (Genesis 16:13). When the eyes of the soul looking out meet the eyes of God looking in, heaven has begun right here on this earth. Nicholas of Cusa wrote four hundred years ago:

> When all my endeavor is turned toward Thee because all Thy endeavor is turned toward me; when I look unto Thee alone with all my attention, nor ever turn aside the eyes of my mind, because Thou dost enfold me with Thy constant regard; when I direct my love toward Thee alone because Thou, who art Love's self hast turned Thee toward me alone. And what, Lord, is my life, save that

embrace wherein Thy delightsome sweetness doth
so lovingly enfold me?[1]

I should like to say more about this old man
of God. He is not much known today anywhere
among Christian believers, and among current fun-
damentalists, he is known not at all. I feel that we
could gain much from a little acquaintance with
men of his spiritual flavor and the school of Christian thought that they represent. Christian literature, to be accepted and approved by evangelical
leaders of our times, must follow very closely the
same train of thought, a kind of "party line" from
which it is scarcely safe to depart. A half-century
of this in America has made us smug and content.
We imitate each other with slavish devotion. Our
most strenuous efforts are put forth to try to say the
same thing that everyone around us is saying—and
yet to find an excuse for saying it, some little safe
variation on the approved theme or, if no more, at
least a new illustration.

Nicholas was a true follower of Christ, a lover
of the Lord, radiant and shining in his devotion to
the person of Jesus. His theology was orthodox but
fragrant and sweet as everything about Jesus might
properly be expected to be. His conception of eternal life, for instance, is beautiful in itself and, if I
mistake not, is nearer in spirit to John 17:3 than that
which is current among us today. Life eternal, says
Nicholas, is

nought other than that blessed regard wherewith Thou never ceasest to behold me, yes, even the secret places of my soul. With Thee, to behold is to give life; 'tis unceasingly to impart sweetest love of Thee; 'tis to inflame me to love of Thee by love's imparting, and to feed me by inflaming, and by feeding to kindle my yearning, and by kindling to make me drink of the dew of gladness, and by drinking to infuse in me a fountain of life, and by infusing to make it increase and endure.[2]

Now, if faith is the gaze of the heart at God, and if this gaze is but the raising of the inward eyes to meet the all-seeing eyes of God, then it follows that it is one of the easiest things possible to do. It would be like God to make the most vital thing easy and place it within the range of possibility for the weakest and poorest of us.

Several conclusions may fairly be drawn from all this. The simplicity of it, for instance. Because believing is looking, it can be done without special equipment or religious paraphernalia. God has seen to it that the one life-and-death essential can never be subject to the caprice of accident. Equipment can break down or get lost, water can leak away, records can be destroyed by fire, the minister can be delayed or the church can burn down. All these are external to the soul and are subject to accident or mechanical failure. But looking is of the heart and can be done successfully by any man standing up or kneeling down or lying in his last agony a thousand miles from any church.

Because believing is looking it can be done any time. No season is superior to another season for this sweetest of all acts. God never made salvation depend upon new moons or holy days or sabbaths. A man is not nearer to Christ on Easter Sunday than he is, say, on Saturday, August 3, or Monday, October 4. As long as Christ sits on the mediatorial throne, every day is a good day and all days are days of salvation.

Neither does place matter to this blessed work of believing God. Lift your heart and let it rest upon Jesus and you are instantly in a sanctuary though it be a Pullman berth or a factory or a kitchen. You can see God from anywhere if your mind is set to love and obey Him.

Now, someone may ask, "Is not this of which you speak for special persons such as monks or ministers who have, by the nature of their calling, more time to devote to quiet meditation? I am a busy worker and have little time to spend alone." I am happy to say that the life I describe is for every one of God's children regardless of calling. It is, in fact, happily practiced every day by many hardworking persons and is beyond the reach of none.

Many have found the secret of which I speak and, without giving much thought to what is going on within them, constantly practice this habit of inwardly gazing upon God. They know that something inside their hearts sees God. Even when they are compelled to withdraw their conscious attention in order to engage in earthly affairs, there is within them a secret communion always going on. Let their attention but be released for a moment from necessary business and it flies at once to God again. This has been the testimony of many Christians, so many that even as I state it thus I have a feeling that I am quoting, though from whom or from how many I cannot possibly know.

I do not want to leave the impression that the ordinary means of grace have no value. They most assuredly have. Private prayer should be practiced by every Christian. Long periods of Bible meditation will purify our gaze and direct it; church attendance will enlarge our outlook and increase our love for others. Service and work and activity—all are good and should be engaged in by every Christian. But at the bottom of all these things, giving meaning to them, will be the inward habit of beholding God. A new set of eyes (so to speak) will develop within us enabling us to be looking at God while our outward eyes are seeing the scenes of this passing world.

Someone may fear that we are magnifying private religion out of all proportion, that the "us" of the New Testament is being displaced by a selfish "I." Has it ever occurred to you that one hundred pianos all tuned to the same fork are automatically tuned to one another? They are of one accord by being tuned, not to one another, but to another standard to which one must individually bow. So one hundred worshippers meeting together, each one looking away to Christ, are in heart nearer to one another than they could possibly be were they to become "unity" conscious and turn their eyes away from God to strive for closer fellowship. Social religion is perfected when private religion is purified. The body becomes stronger as its members become healthier. The whole church of God gains when the members who compose it begin to seek a better and a higher life.

All the foregoing presupposes true repentance and a full committal of the life to God. It is hardly necessary to mention this, for only persons who have made such a committal will have read this far.

When the habit of inwardly gazing Godward becomes fixed within us, we shall be ushered onto a new level of spiritual life more in keeping with the promises of God and the mood of the New Testament. The Triune God will be our dwelling place even while our feet walk the low road of simple duty here among men. We will have found life's summum bonum indeed.

> There is the source of all delights that can be desired; not only can nought better be thought out by men and angels, but nought better can exist in any mode of being! For it is the absolute maximum of every rational desire, than which a greater cannot be.[3]

O Lord, I have heard a good word inviting me to look away to Thee and be satisfied. My heart longs to respond, but sin has clouded my vision till I see Thee but dimly. Be pleased to cleanse me in Thine own precious blood, and make me inwardly pure, so that I may with unveiled eyes gaze upon Thee all the days of my earthly pilgrimage. Then shall I be prepared to behold Thee in full splendor in the day when Thou shalt appear to be glorified in Thy saints and admired in all them that believe. Amen.

Questions for Reflection
The Gaze of the Soul

1. "Without faith it is impossible to please [God]" (Hebrews 11:6). "Faith will get me anything, take me anywhere in the kingdom of God, but without faith there can be no approach to God, no forgiveness, no deliverance, no salvation, no communion, no spiritual life at all." Where do we start the process of building our faith? What resources are available to help us?

2. In Hebrews 11:1 "faith is functionally defined, not philosophically; that is, it is a statement of what faith is in operation, not what it is in essence. It assumes the presence of faith and shows what it results in, rather than what it is." Basically, Tozer concludes that "faith is the gaze of a soul upon the saving God." Reflect on or discuss this definition of faith. Share some situations where you know for sure that you walked by faith.

3. From Hebrews 12:2, "we learn that faith is not a once-done act, but a continuous gaze of the heart at the Triune God." The easiest way to assess whether or not we have a continuous gaze of the soul on God is to reflect on or evaluate the last twenty-four hours, the last week and the last month of our walk with the Lord. Has the gaze been continuous, broken, almost

non-existent or not at all? If the gaze of your soul on God has not been what it should be, confess and forsake your sins, recommit your entire life to Christ in faith and resume a constant gaze upon God. Do not be afraid to get help from a more mature believer in learning to practice the presence of God.

4. "If faith is the gaze of the heart at God, and if this gaze is but the raising of the inward eyes to meet the all-seeing eyes of God," then it is a simple act that can be done anytime and anyplace. Has this inward habit of beholding God become a continual part of your day? If not, what's stopping you?

5. The believer who wants to please God is preoccupied with Him, not self, but he is also aware that he does not have the power within himself to walk by faith (Zechariah 4:6). Any self-effort will fail. If you truly want to experience a biblical walk of faith, consider praying this prayer for a new beginning:

O Lord God, I desire a continuous gaze of my heart at the Triune God; but my own sin, the unclean culture I live in, the tremendous emphasis on doing instead of being in Christ and the fast pace of dashing to and fro through life have blinded me to Your majesty, Your perfections and Your total sufficiency for all my needs. Open my eyes anew that I may behold Thee all my days, so that one day I will hear, "Well done, good and faithful servant" as a result of walking by faith from this day forward. As I am occupied with Thee, I will walk by faith in the good works which You prepared beforehand, bringing glory to Your name, not mine. Amen.

Key to Original Sources

Title of original book is followed by the number(s) of the essay(s) that is(are) from that book.

The Attributes of God, Volume 2: 2

Born After Midnight: 7, 26

Faith Beyond Reason: 5

God's Pursuit of Man: 4

God Tells the Man Who Cares: 17, 24

Man: The Dwelling Place of God: 14, 15, 18

Of God and Men: 13, 19, 21, 25, 29

The Pursuit of God: 1, 3, 27, 30

The Root of the Righteous: 6, 8, 9, 11, 22, 23, 28

Rut, Rot or Revival: 10

That Incredible Christian: 20

The Warfare of the Spirit: 12, 16

Notes

Chapter 2

[1] Alfred Lord Tennyson, *Morte d'Arthur*.

[2] John Milton, *Paradise Lost*, First Book.

[3] John Milton, *Paradise Lost*, First Book.

[4] Frederick William Faber, "Majesty Divine!" in A.W. Tozer, compiler, *The Christian Book of Mystical Verse* (Camp Hill, PA: WingSpread Publishers, 1963, 1991), p. 7.

[5] Ibid.

Chapter 30

[1] Nicholas of Cusa, *The Vision of God*, (New York: E.P. Dutton & Co., Inc., 1928.) Used by kind permission of the publishers.

[2] Ibid.

[3] Ibid.

About the Compiler

Dr. W.L. Seaver is an associate professor of statistics at the University of Tennessee. He holds a Ph.D. in Statistics, a Master of Business Administration and a Master of Arts in Biblical Studies. He is the author of *A Mosaic of Faith: 11 Lessons Jesus Taught His Disciples* (WingSpread Publishers, 2012), more than thirty articles and is also a researcher and consultant whose expertise is in finding patterns in data and the Scriptures over time. He has developed discipleship ministries with athletes, students, faculty and the community church. He and his wife, Barbara, have three grown children.

Other Titles by A.W. Tozer

**The following titles are also
available as audio CDs,
unabridged editions:**